Congressional
Research
Service

Congressional Oversight and Related Issues Concerning International Security Agreements Concluded by the United States

Michael John Garcia
Legislative Attorney

R. Chuck Mason
Legislative Attorney

June 7, 2012

Congressional Research Service

7-5700

www.crs.gov

R40614

CRS Report for Congress

Prepared for Members and Committees of Congress

Summary

The United States is a party to numerous security agreements with other nations. The topics covered, along with the significance of the obligations imposed upon agreement parties, may vary. Some international security agreements entered by the United States, such as those obliging parties to come to the defense of another in the event of an attack, involve substantial commitments and have traditionally been entered as treaties, ratified with the advice and consent of the Senate. Other agreements dealing with more technical matters, such as military basing rights or the application of a host country's laws to U.S. forces stationed within, are entered more routinely and usually take a form other than treaty (i.e., as an executive agreement or a nonlegal political commitment).

Occasionally, the substance and form of a proposed security agreement may become a source of dispute between Congress and the executive branch. In late 2007, the Bush Administration announced its intention to negotiate a long-term security agreement with Iraq that would have committed the United States to provide security assurances to Iraq and maintain a long-term military presence in that country. This announcement became a source of congressional interest, in part because of statements by Administration officials that such an agreement would not be submitted to the legislative branch for approval. Congressional concern dissipated when U.S.-Iraq negotiations culminated in an agreement that did not contain a long-term security commitment by the United States, but instead called for the withdrawal of U.S. forces from Iraq by December 31, 2011.

On May 2, 2012, President Barack Obama and President Hamid Karzai signed the Enduring Strategic Partnership Agreement Between the United States of America and the Islamic Republic of Afghanistan. Under the terms of the Agreement, the parties pledge to work cooperatively in a number of fields, including to promote shared democratic values, advance long-term security, reinforce regional security, advance social and economic development, and strengthen Afghan institutions and governance. Additionally, the Agreement provides that the United States and Afghanistan shall initiate negotiations on a Bilateral Security Agreement (with the goal of concluding such an agreement within a year), which is intended to replace the existing agreement relating to the status of military and civilian personnel currently in Afghanistan.

It is likely that future disputes will arise between the political branches regarding the entering or implementation of international security agreements. Regardless of the form a security arrangement may take, Congress has several tools to exercise oversight regarding the negotiation, form, conclusion, and implementation of the agreement by the United States. This report begins by providing a general background on the types of international agreements that are binding upon the United States, as well as considerations affecting whether they take the form of a treaty or an executive agreement. Next, the report discusses historical precedents as to the role that security agreements have taken, with specific attention paid to past agreements entered with Afghanistan, Germany, Japan, South Korea, the Philippines, and Iraq. The report discusses the oversight role that Congress exercises with respect to entering and implementing international agreements involving the United States.

Contents

I. International Agreements Under U.S. Law 1
  Treaties 1
  Executive Agreements 2
    Congressional-Executive Agreements 4
    Executive Agreements Made Pursuant to Treaties 5
    Sole Executive Agreements 5
    Nonlegal Agreements 7
    Choosing Between a Treaty and Executive Agreement 8
II. Historical Practice Regarding Security Agreements 9
  Categories of Security Agreements 9
    Collective Defense Agreements/"Security Commitments" 10
    Consultation Requirements/"Security Arrangements" 11
    Other Types of Military Agreements 12
    Agreements Granting the Legal Right to Military Intervention 13
  Non-Binding Security Arrangements 14
  Examples of Bilateral Security Agreements 16
    Afghanistan 16
    Iraq 20
    Germany 22
    Japan 23
    South Korea 24
    Philippines 26
III. Congressional Oversight 27
  Notification 27
    Notification Pursuant to the Case-Zablocki Act 27
    Notification Pursuant to Circular 175 Procedures 28
    Annual Reporting of Security Arrangements Required by the National Defense
      Authorization Act of 1991 28
  Consultation 29
  Approval, Rejection, or Conditional Approval of International Agreements 30
  Implementation of an Agreement That Is Not Self-Executing 31
  Continuing Oversight 31

Contacts

Author Contact Information 32

The United States is a party to numerous security agreements with other nations. The topics covered, along with the significance of the obligations imposed upon agreement parties, may vary. Some international security agreements entered by the United States, such as those obliging parties to come to the defense of another in the event of an attack, involve substantial commitments and have traditionally been entered as treaties, ratified with the advice and consent of the Senate. Other agreements dealing with more technical matters, such as military basing rights or the application of a host country's laws to U.S. forces stationed within, are entered more routinely and usually take a form other than treaty.

Regardless of the form of a security arrangement, Congress has several tools which enable it to exercise oversight regarding the negotiation, form, conclusion, and implementation of the agreement by the United States. This report begins by providing a general background as to the types of international agreements that are binding upon the United States, as well as considerations affecting whether they take the form of a treaty or an executive agreement. Next, the report examines historical precedents, with specific attention paid to past agreements entered with Afghanistan, Iraq, Germany, Japan, South Korea, and the Philippines. Finally, the report discusses the oversight role that Congress exercises with respect to entering and implementing international agreements involving the United States.

I. International Agreements Under U.S. Law

Under U.S. law, a legally binding international agreement can be entered into pursuant to either a treaty or an executive agreement. The Constitution allocates primary responsibility for entering such agreements to the executive branch, but Congress also plays an essential role. First, in order for a treaty (but not an executive agreement) to become the "Law of the Land,"[1] the Senate must provide its advice and consent to treaty ratification by a two-thirds majority. Alternatively, Congress may authorize congressional-executive agreements. Many treaties and executive agreements are not "self-executing," meaning that in order for them to take effect domestically, implementing legislation is required to provide U.S. bodies with the authority necessary to enforce and comply with the agreements' provisions. While some executive agreements do not require congressional approval, adherence to them may nonetheless be dependent upon Congress appropriating necessary funds or authorizing the activities to be carried out (where compliance with the agreement would contravene some statutory provision).

Treaties

Under U.S. law, a treaty is an agreement negotiated and signed[2] by the executive branch, which enters into force if it is approved by a two-thirds majority in the Senate and is subsequently

---

[1] U.S. CONST., art. VI, §2. In this regard, it is important to distinguish "treaty" in the context of international law, in which "treaty" and "international agreement" are synonymous terms for all binding agreements, and "treaty" in the context of domestic U.S. law, in which "treaty" more narrowly refers to a particular subcategory of binding international agreements. It should be noted, however, that the term "treaty" is not always interpreted under U.S. law to refer only to those agreements described in Article II, §2 of the Constitution. *See Weinberger v. Rossi*, 456 U.S. 25 (1982) (interpreting statute barring discrimination except where permitted by "treaty" to refer to both treaties and executive agreements); *B. Altman & Co. v. United States*, 224 U.S. 583 (1912) (construing the term "treaty," as used in statute conferring appellate jurisdiction, to also refer to executive agreements).

[2] Under international law, States (i.e., countries) that have signed but not ratified treaties have the obligation to refrain from acts that would defeat the object or purpose of the treaty. Vienna Convention on the Law of Treaties, entered into (continued...)

---

ratified following presidential signature.[3] The Senate may, in considering a treaty, condition its consent on certain reservations,[4] declarations,[5] and understandings[6] concerning treaty application. If accepted, these reservations, declarations, and understandings may limit and/or define U.S. obligations under the treaty.[7]

Executive Agreements

The great majority of international agreements that the United States enters into are not treaties but executive agreements[8]—agreements made by the executive branch that are not submitted to the Senate for its advice and consent. There are three types of *prima facie* legal executive agreements: (1) *congressional-executive agreements*, in which Congress has previously or retroactively authorized an international agreement entered into by the executive; (2) *executive agreements made pursuant to an earlier treaty*, in which the agreement is authorized by a ratified treaty; and (3) *sole executive agreements*, in which an agreement is made pursuant to the President's constitutional authority without further congressional authorization. The executive's authority to promulgate the agreement is different in each case.

Although executive agreements are not specifically discussed in the Constitution, they nonetheless have been considered valid international compacts under Supreme Court jurisprudence and as a matter of historical practice.[9] Starting in the World War II era, reliance on

---

(...continued)

force January 27, 1980, 1155 U.N.T.S. 331 [hereinafter "Vienna Convention"], art. 18. Although the United States has not ratified the Vienna Convention, it recognizes it as generally expressing customary international law. *See, e.g., Fujitsu Ltd. v. Federal Exp. Corp.*, 247 F.3d 423, 433 (2nd Cir. 2001) ("we rely upon the Vienna Convention here as an authoritative guide to the customary international law of treaties ... [b]ecause the United States recognizes the Vienna Convention as a codification of customary international law ... and [it] acknowledges the Vienna Convention as, in large part, the authoritative guide to current treaty law and practice") (internal citations omitted).

[3] Oftentimes, a bilateral treaty will only come into effect after the parties exchange instruments of ratification. In the case of multilateral treaties, ratification typically occurs only after the treaty's instruments of ratification are submitted to the appropriate body in accordance with the terms of the agreement.

[4] A "reservation" is "a unilateral statement ... made by a State, when signing, ratifying, accepting, approving or acceding to a treaty, whereby it purports to exclude or to modify the legal effect of certain provisions of the treaty in their application to that State." Vienna Convention, art. 2(1)(d). In practice, "[r]eservations change U.S. obligations without necessarily changing the text, and they require the acceptance of the other party." CONGRESSIONAL RESEARCH SERVICE, TREATIES AND OTHER INTERNATIONAL AGREEMENTS: THE ROLE OF THE UNITED STATES SENATE, A STUDY PREPARED FOR THE SENATE COMM. ON FOREIGN RELATIONS 11 (Comm. Print 2001); Vienna Convention, arts. 19-23.

[5] Declarations are "statements expressing the Senate's position or opinion on matters relating to issues raised by the treaty rather than to specific provisions." TREATIES AND OTHER INTERNATIONAL AGREEMENTS, *supra* note 4, at 11.

[6] Understandings are "interpretive statements that clarify or elaborate provisions but do not alter them." *Id.*

[7] As a matter of customary international law, States are "obliged to refrain from acts which would defeat the object and purpose of a treaty," including entering reservations that are incompatible with a treaty's purposes. Vienna Convention, arts. 18-19.

[8] LOUIS HENKIN, FOREIGN AFFAIRS AND THE U.S. CONSTITUTION 215 (2nd ed. 1996).

[9] *E.g., American Ins. Ass'n v. Garamendi*, 539 U.S. 396, 415 (2003) ("our cases have recognized that the President has authority to make 'executive agreements' with other countries, requiring no ratification by the Senate ... this power having been exercised since the early years of the Republic"); *United States v. Belmont*, 301 U.S. 324, 330 ("an international compact ... is not always a treaty which requires the participation of the Senate").

---

executive agreements has grown significantly,[10] with the number of international agreements entered as executive agreements significantly dwarfing those entered as treaties.[11]

Although some have argued that certain agreements may only be entered as treaties, subject to the advice and consent of the Senate,[12] this view has been rejected by many scholars.[13] Adjudication of the propriety of executive agreements has been rare, in significant part because plaintiffs often cannot demonstrate that they have suffered a redressable injury giving them standing to challenge an agreement,[14] or fail to make a justiciable claim. In 2001, the Eleventh Circuit Court of Appeals held that the issue of whether the North American Free Trade Agreement (NAFTA) was a treaty

---

[10] TREATIES AND OTHER INTERNATIONAL AGREEMENTS, *supra* note 4, at 38-40.

[11] According to one estimate, between 1789 and 2004, the United States entered 1,834 treaties and 16,704 executive agreements, meaning that roughly 10% of agreements concluded by the United States during that period took the form of treaties. WILLIAM R. SLOMANSON, FUNDAMENTAL PERSPECTIVES ON INTERNATIONAL LAW 376 (5ᵗʰ ed. 2007). This number may not take into account the numerous minor or technical agreements entered by the United States each year, which are often entered to implement more general provisions found in treaties or executive agreements. *Cf.* 21 C.F.R. §181.2(a)(2) (interpreting Case-Zablocki Act, 1 U.S.C. §112b, which requires congressional notification of international agreements other than treaties which enter into force for the United States, and 1 U.S.C. §112a, requiring the publishing of international agreements to which the United States is a party, to not cover "minor or trivial undertakings, even if couched in legal language and form").

[12] *E.g.*, Edwin Borchard, *Treaties and Executive Agreements A Reply*, 54 YALE L. J. 616 (1945) (arguing that the congressional-executive agreement is not a constitutionally permissible alternative to a treaty, and that sole executive agreements are permissible in limited circumstances); Bradford C. Clark, *Domesticating Sole Executive Agreements*, 93 VA. L. REV. 1573 (2007) (arguing that the text and drafting history of the Constitution supports the position that treaties and executive agreements are not interchangeable, and also arguing that the Supremacy Clause should be read to generally preclude sole executive agreements from overriding existing law); Laurence H. Tribe, *Taking Text and Structure Seriously Reflections on Free-Form Method in Constitutional Interpretation*, 108 HARV. L. REV. 1221 (1995) (arguing that the Treaty Clause is the exclusive means for Congress to approve significant international agreements); John C. Yoo, *Laws as Treaties? the Constitutionality of Congressional-Executive Agreements*, 99 MICH. L. REV. 757 (2001) (arguing that treaties are the constitutionally required form for congressional approval of an international agreement concerning action lying outside of Congress's constitutional powers, including matters with respect to human rights, political/military alliances, and arms control, but are not required for agreements concerning action falling within Congress's powers under Art. I of the Constitution, such as agreements concerning international commerce).

[13] RESTATEMENT (THIRD) OF FOREIGN RELATIONS, §303 n.8 (1987) ("At one time it was argued that some agreements can be made only as treaties, by the procedure designated in the Constitution.... Scholarly opinion has rejected that view."); HENKIN, *supra* note 8, at 217 ("Whatever their theoretical merits, it is now widely accepted that the Congressional-Executive agreement is available for wide use, even general use, and is a complete alternative to a treaty...."); Yoo, *supra* note 12, at 759 (noting that "a broad intellectual consensus exists that congressional-executive agreements may serve as full substitutes for treaties"); Oona A. Hathaway, *Treaties' End The Past, Present, And Future Of International Lawmaking In The United States*, 117 YALE L.J. 1236, 1244 (2008) (noting that "weight of scholarly opinion" since the 1940s has been in favor of the view that treaties and congressional-executive agreements are interchangeable). *Cf.* Bruce Ackerman & David Golove, *Is NAFTA Constitutional?*, 108 HARV. L. REV. 799 (1995) (arguing that developments in the World War II era altered historical understanding of the Constitution's allocation of power between government branches so as to make congressional-executive agreement a complete alternative to a treaty); Myres S. McDougal and Asher Lans, *Treaties and Congressional-Executive or Presidential Agreements Interchangeable Instruments of National Policy* (parts I and II), 54 YALE L. J. 181, 534 (1945) (arguing that historical practice supports the interchangeability of congressional-executive agreements and treaties).

[14] RESTATEMENT, *supra* note 13, at §302, n. 5; HENKIN, *supra* note 8, at 142-148. *See also Greater Tampa Chamber of Commerce v. Goldschmidt*, 627 F.2d 258 (D.C. Cir. 1980) (finding that plaintiffs lacked standing to challenge the propriety of the form taken by an international agreement between the United States and United Kingdom). Executive agreements dealing with matters having no direct impact upon private interests in the United States (e.g., agreements concerning military matters or foreign relations) are rarely the subject of domestic litigation, in part because persons typically cannot demonstrate that they have suffered an actual, redressable injury and therefore lack standing to challenge such agreements. RESTATEMENT, *supra* note 13, at §303, n. 11.

---

requiring approval by two-thirds of the Senate presented a nonjusticiable political question.[15] It does not appear that an executive agreement has ever been held invalid by the courts on the grounds that it was in contravention of the Treaty Clause.[16] Nonetheless, as a matter of historical practice, some types of agreements have been concluded as treaties, while others have been concluded as executive agreements.[17]

Congressional-Executive Agreements

In the case of congressional-executive agreements, the "constitutionality ... seems well established."[18] Unlike treaties, where only the Senate plays a role in authorization, both houses of Congress are involved in the authorizing process for congressional-executive agreements. Congressional authorization takes the form of a statute passed by a majority of both houses of Congress. Historically, congressional-executive agreements cover a wide variety of topics, ranging from postal conventions to bilateral trade to military assistance.[19] NAFTA and the General Agreement on Tariffs and Trade (GATT) are notable examples of congressional-executive agreements.

Congressional-executive agreements also may take different forms. Congress may enact legislation authorizing the executive to negotiate and enter agreements with other countries on a specific matter.[20] A congressional-executive agreement may also take the form of a statute passed following the negotiation of an agreement which incorporates the terms or requirements of the agreement into U.S. law.[21] Such authorization may be either explicit or implied by the terms of the congressional enactment.[22]

---

[15] *Made in the USA Foundation v. United States*, 242 F.3d 1300 (11ᵗʰ Cir. 2001), cert. denied by *United Steelworkers of America, AFL-CIO, CLC v. United States*, 534 U.S. 1039 (2001).

[16] In 1997, a federal district court in Texas ruled petitioner was not extraditable pursuant to a federal statute implementing an executive agreement, and held that extradition requires an extradition treaty ratified by the President and approved by two-thirds of the Senate. *In re* Surrender of Ntakirutimana, 988 F.Supp. 1038 (S.D.Tex. 1997). The Fifth Circuit Court of Appeals overturned the district court's finding and held that a person could be extradited by statute rather than treaty. *Ntakirutimana v. Reno*, 184 F.3d 419 (5ᵗʰ Cir. 1999), *cert. denied by* 528 U.S. 1135 (2000).

[17] *See* Yoo, *supra* note 12 (discussing the kinds of agreements historically taking the form of treaties in contrast to those taking the form of executive agreements). *See also infra* pp. 9-15 (discussing form that different types of U.S. security agreements have historically taken).

[18] TREATIES AND OTHER INTERNATIONAL AGREEMENTS, *supra* note 4, at 5. *See also* HENKIN, *supra* note 8, at 215-18.

[19] TREATIES AND OTHER INTERNATIONAL AGREEMENTS, *supra* note 4, at 5. Reciprocal trade agreements which were once concluded as treaties now typically take the form of congressional-executive agreements. RESTATEMENT, *supra* note 13, at §303, n. 9. *See also* 19 U.S.C. §2111 (conditionally authorizing the President to enter trade agreements with other nations); CRS Report 97-896, *Why Certain Trade Agreements Are Approved as Congressional-Executive Agreements Rather Than as Treaties*, by Jeanne J. Grimmett.

[20] *See, e.g.*, 16 U.S.C. §1822(a) (authorizing the Secretary of State to negotiate international fishery agreements); 22 U.S.C. §6445(c) (authorizing the President to enter binding agreements with other nations pledging to end practices violating religious freedom).

[21] *See, e.g.*, 19 U.S.C. §3511 (approving agreements resulting from the Uruguay Round of multilateral trade negotiations under the auspices of GATT).

[22] *See, e.g.*, 19 U.S.C. §3471 (authorizing U.S. participation in and appropriations for Commission on Labor Cooperation, established by a supplemental NAFTA agreement not expressly approved by Congress).

Executive Agreements Made Pursuant to Treaties

The legitimacy of agreements made pursuant to treaties is also well established, though controversy occasionally arises as to whether the agreement was actually imputed by the treaty in question.[23] Since the earlier treaty is the "Law of the Land,"[24] the power to enter into an agreement required or contemplated by the treaty lies fairly clearly within the President's executive function. However, the Senate occasionally conditions its approval of a treaty upon a requirement that any subsequent agreement made pursuant to the treaty also be submitted to the Senate as a treaty.[25]

Sole Executive Agreements

Sole executive agreements rely on neither treaty nor congressional authority for their legal basis. There are a number of provisions in the Constitution that may confer limited authority upon the President to promulgate such agreements on the basis of his power to conduct foreign affairs.[26] The Litvinov Assignment, under which the Soviet Union purported to transfer claims against American assets previously nationalized by the Soviet Union, is an example of a sole executive agreement.

If the President enters into an executive agreement pursuant to and dealing with an area where he has clear, exclusive constitutional authority—such as an agreement to recognize a particular state for diplomatic purposes—the agreement is legally permissible regardless of Congress's opinion on the matter.[27] If, however, the President enters into an agreement and his constitutional authority over the subject matter is unclear, or if Congress also has constitutional authority over the subject matter, a reviewing court may consider Congress's position in determining whether the agreement is enforceable as U.S. law.[28] If Congress has given implicit approval to the President to enter into the agreement, or is silent on the matter, a reviewing court might be more likely to view the agreement as valid.[29] When Congress opposes the agreement and the

---

[23] TREATIES AND OTHER INTERNATIONAL AGREEMENTS, *supra* note 4, at 5.

[24] U.S. CONST. art. VI, §2 ("the laws of the United States ... [and] all treaties made, or which shall be made, under the authority of the United States, shall be the supreme Law of the Land").

[25] *See* RESTATEMENT, *supra* note 25, §303 cmt. d.

[26] U.S. CONST. art. II, §1 ("The executive power shall be vested in a President of the United States of America ..."), §2 ("The President shall be commander in chief of the Army and Navy of the United States ..."), §3 ("he shall receive ambassadors and other public ministers ..."). Courts have recognized foreign affairs as an area of very strong executive authority. *See United States v. Curtiss-Wright Export Corp.*, 299 U.S. 304 (1936).

[27] *See* RESTATEMENT, *supra* note 13, §303 (4).

[28] *See Dames & Moore v. Regan*, 453 U.S. 654 (1981) (establishing that Congress's implicit approval of executive action, such as historical practice of yielding authority in a particular area, may legitimize an agreement); *Youngstown Sheet & Tube Co. v. Sawyer*, 343 U.S. 579 (1952) ("When the President acts pursuant to an express or implied authorization of Congress, his powers are at their maximum.... Congressional inertia, indifference or quiescence may ... invite, measures of independent Presidential responsibility.... When the President takes measures incompatible with the expressed or implied will of Congress, his power is at its lowest ebb, for then he can rely only upon his own constitutional powers minus any constitutional powers of Congress over the matter.") (Jackson, J., concurring).

[29] *See* citations accompanying note 28. *But see* Medellin v. Texas, 552 U.S. 491, 531-532 (2008) (suggesting that *Dames & Moore* analysis regarding significance of congressional acquiescence might be relevant only in a "narrow set of circumstances," where presidential action is supported by a "particularly longstanding practice" of congressional acquiescence).

President's constitutional authority to enter the agreement is ambiguous, it is unclear if or under what circumstances a court would recognize such an agreement as controlling.

Because sole executive agreements do not rely on congressional authority to support their legality, they do not require congressional approval to become binding, at least as a matter of international law. Courts have recognized, however, that if a sole executive agreement conflicts with preexisting federal law, the earlier law will remain controlling in most circumstances.[30]

Even if a sole executive agreement does not conflict with prior federal law, Congress may still act to limit the agreement's effect through a subsequent legislative enactment, so long as it has constitutional authority to regulate the matter covered by the agreement.[31] In the security context, Congress has clear constitutional authority to enact measures that would limit the effect of sole executive agreements involving military commitments. Article I, Section 8 of the Constitution accords Congress the power "To lay and collect Taxes ... to ... pay the Debts and provide for the common Defence," "To declare War, grant letters of Marque and Reprisal, and make Rules concerning Captures on Land and Water," "To raise and support Armies," "To provide and maintain a Navy," "To make Rules for the Government and Regulation of the land and naval Forces," as well as "To provide for calling forth the Militia to execute the Laws of the Union, suppress Insurrections and repel Invasions" and "To provide for organizing, arming, and disciplining, the Militia, and for governing such Part of them as may be employed in the Service of the United States."[32] Further, Congress is empowered "To make all Laws which shall be necessary and proper for carrying into Execution the foregoing Powers" as well as "all other Powers vested by this Constitution in the Government of the United States, or in any Department or Officer thereof."[33]

In addition to the constitutional provisions that provide Congress with authority to legislate on matters concerning military affairs,[34] Congress also has virtual plenary power over appropriations—authority not qualified with reference to Congress's enumerated powers under Article I, Section 8. The Appropriations Clause provides that "[n]o money can be paid out of the Treasury unless it has been appropriated by an act of Congress."[35] Accordingly, adherence to

---

[30] Executive agreements have been held to be inferior to conflicting federal law when the agreement concerns matters expressly within the constitutional authority of Congress. *See, e.g., United States v. Guy W. Capps, Inc.*, 204 F.2d 655 (4th Cir. 1953) (finding that executive agreement contravening provisions of import statute was unenforceable); RESTATEMENT, *supra* note 13, §115, n.5. However, an executive agreement might trump preexisting federal law if it concerns an enumerated or inherent executive power under the Constitution, or if Congress has historically acquiesced to the President entering agreements in the relevant area. *See id.; United States v. Pink*, 315 U.S. 203, 230 (1942) ("[a]ll Constitutional acts of power, whether in the executive or in the judicial department, have as much legal validity and obligation as if they proceeded from the legislature") (quoting THE FEDERALIST NO. 64 (John Jay)); *Dames & Moore*, 453 U.S. at 654 (upholding sole executive agreement concerning the handling of Iranian assets in the United States, despite the existence of a potentially conflicting statute, given Congress's historical acquiescence to these types of agreements). *But see Medellin*, 552 U.S. at 531-532 (suggesting that sole executive agreements may create domestically enforceable law in a limited number of areas). *See also* Clark, *supra* note 12 (discussing and criticizing development of pre-*Medellin* jurisprudence recognizing domestic legal effect of sole executive agreements).

[31] The "last in time" rule establishes that a more recent statute trumps an earlier, inconsistent international agreement, while a more recent self-executing agreement may trump an earlier, inconsistent statute. *Whitney v. Robertson*, 124 U.S. 190 (1888).

[32] U.S. CONST. art. I, §8.

[33] *Id.*

[34] For additional discussion, see CRS Report R41989, *Congressional Authority to Limit Military Operations*, by Jennifer K. Elsea, Michael John Garcia, and Thomas J. Nicola.

[35] U.S. CONST. art. I, §9. Congress may specify the terms and conditions under which appropriations may be used, so (continued...)

---

pledges made in sole executive agreements may be dependent upon the availability of appropriations authorized by Congress. Congress may specify the terms and conditions under which appropriations may be used, so long as it does not impose unconstitutional conditions upon the use of appropriated funds.[36]

Nonlegal Agreements

Not every pledge, assurance, or arrangement made between the United States and a foreign party constitutes a legally binding international agreement. In some cases, the United States makes "political commitments" or "gentlemen's agreements" with foreign states. Although these commitments are nonlegal, they may nonetheless carry significant moral and political weight.[37] The executive has long claimed the authority to enter such agreements on behalf of the United States without congressional authorization, asserting that the entering of political commitments by the executive is not subject to the same constitutional constraints as the entering of legally binding international agreements.[38] An example of a nonlegal agreement is the 1975 Helsinki Accords, a Cold War agreement signed by 35 nations, which contains provisions concerning territorial integrity, human rights, scientific and economic cooperation, peaceful settlement of disputes, and the implementation of confidence-building measures.

An international agreement is generally presumed to be legally binding in the absence of an express provision indicating its nonlegal nature. State Department regulations recognize that this presumption may be overcome when there is "clear evidence, in the negotiating history of the agreement or otherwise, that the parties intended the arrangement to be governed by another legal system."[39] Other factors that may be relevant in determining whether an agreement is nonlegal in nature include the form of the agreement and the specificity of its provisions.[40]

(...continued)

long as it does not impose unconstitutional conditions on the use of appropriated funds.

[36] *See United States v. Klein*, 80 U.S. (8 Wall.) 128 (1872) (holding invalid an appropriations proviso that effectively nullified some effects of a presidential pardon and that appeared to prescribe a rule of decision in court cases); *United States v. Lovett*, 328 U.S. 303 (1946)(invalidating as a bill of attainder an appropriations provision denying money to pay salaries of named officials). For further discussion of Congress's ability to use its appropriations power to limit the deployment or use of U.S. military forces, see CRS Report R41989, *Congressional Authority to Limit Military Operations*, by Jennifer K. Elsea, Michael John Garcia, and Thomas J. Nicola.

[37] *See generally* Kal Raustiala, *Compliance & Effectiveness in International Regulatory Cooperation*, 32 CASE W. RES. J. INT'L L. 387, 423-427 (2000) (discussing advantages of nonlegal agreements, and suggesting that they may occasionally facilitate greater changes in countries' behavior than binding agreements); Oscar Schachter, Editorial Comment, *The Twilight Existence of Nonbinding International Agreements*, 71 AM. J. INT'L L. 296 (1977) (discussing significance of nonlegal agreements in international practice).

[38] *See generally* Robert E. Dalton, Asst. Legal Adviser for Treaty Affairs, *International Documents of a Non-Legally Binding Character*, State Department, Memorandum, March 18, 1994, available at http://www.state.gov/documents/organization/65728.pdf (discussing U.S. and international practice with respect to nonlegal, political agreements); Duncan B. Hollis and Joshua J. Newcomer, *"Political" Commitments and the Constitution*, 49 VA. J. INT'L L. 507 (2009) (discussing U.S. political commitments made to foreign States and the constitutional implications of the practice).

[39] 22 C.F.R. §181.2(a).

[40] *Id. See also infra* at "Notification Pursuant to the Case-Zablocki Act"; State Department Office of the Legal Adviser, *Guidance on Non-Binding Documents*, at http://www.state.gov/s/l/treaty/guidance/.

Choosing Between a Treaty and Executive Agreement

A recurring concern for the executive and legislative branches is whether an international commitment should be entered into as a treaty or an executive agreement. The Senate may prefer that significant international commitments be entered as treaties, and fear that reliance on executive agreements will lead to an erosion of the treaty power. The House may want an international compact to take the form of a congressional-executive agreement, so that it may play a greater role in its consideration. In cases where congressional action is necessary for an agreement to be implemented, the executive may prefer to submit an international compact as a congressional-executive agreement, so that approval of the agreement and the enactment of necessary implementing legislation may be accomplished in a single step. The executive's preference as to whether an international compact takes the form of a treaty or executive agreement may also be influenced by the agreement's prospects for approval by a two-thirds majority of the Senate or a simple majority of both houses.

State Department regulations prescribing the process for coordination and approval of international agreements (commonly known as the "Circular 175 procedure")[41] include criteria for determining whether an international agreement should take the form of a treaty or an executive agreement. Congressional preference is one of several factors considered when determining the form that an international agreement should take. According to State Department regulations,

> In determining a question as to the procedure which should be followed for any particular international agreement, due consideration is given to the following factors:
>
> (1) The extent to which the agreement involves commitments or risks affecting the nation as a whole;
>
> (2) Whether the agreement is intended to affect state laws;
>
> (3) Whether the agreement can be given effect without the enactment of subsequent legislation by the Congress;
>
> (4) Past U.S. practice as to similar agreements;
>
> (5) The preference of the Congress as to a particular type of agreement;
>
> (6) The degree of formality desired for an agreement;
>
> (7) The proposed duration of the agreement, the need for prompt conclusion of an agreement, and the desirability of concluding a routine or short-term agreement; and
>
> (8) The general international practice as to similar agreements.
>
> In determining whether any international agreement should be brought into force as a treaty or as an international agreement other than a treaty, the utmost care is to be exercised to

---

[41] Circular 175 initially referred to a 1955 Department of State Circular which established a process for the coordination and approval of international agreements. These procedures, as modified, are now found in 22 CFR part 181 and 11 Foreign Affairs Manual (F.A.M.) chapter 720.

avoid any invasion or compromise of the constitutional powers of the President, the Senate, and the Congress as a whole.[42]

In 1978, the Senate passed a resolution expressing its sense that the President seek the advice of the Senate Committee on Foreign Relations in determining whether an international agreement should be submitted as a treaty.[43] The State Department subsequently modified the Circular 175 procedure to provide for consultation with appropriate congressional leaders and committees concerning significant international agreements.[44] Consultations are to be held "as appropriate."[45] Congressional consultation on the substance and form of international agreements is discussed in more detail later in this report.[46]

II. Historical Practice Regarding Security Agreements

The following sections provide a general overview of the categories of security agreements entered into by the United States of a legally binding nature. Such categories of security agreements predominantly take the form of a treaty, while others typically take the form of an executive agreement.

Categories of Security Agreements

Although some categories of security agreements have historically been entered as treaties and others as executive agreements, this does not necessarily mean that future arrangements must follow the same pattern. Arguably, an arrangement that has typically been entered into as a treaty might instead take the form of a congressional-executive agreement, and vice versa.[47] Similarly, while some security arrangements have historically been entered as sole executive agreements, Congress might effectively limit such agreements in the future via statutory enactment[48]—for

---

[42] 11 F.A.M. §723.3 (2006).

[43] S.Res. 536, S.Rept. 95-1171, 95th Cong. (1977).

[44] 11 F.A.M. §724.4(b)-(c) (2006).

[45] *Id.* at §724.4(c).

[46] *See infra* at 27.

[47] In 1976, the Senate gave its advice and consent to ratification of the Treaty of Friendship and Cooperation with Spain, 27 U.S.T. 3005 (entered into force September 21, 1976), which included provisions relating to U.S. basing rights and the status of U.S. forces in Spain. Following the end of the Franco regime and Spain becoming a member of NATO, the United States concluded an executive agreement with Spain which was of similar scope to the 1976 treaty. Agreement on Friendship, Defense and Cooperation Between the United States and Spain, with Complementary Agreements, 34 U.S.T. 3885, entered into force May 14, 1983. *But see* Yoo, *supra* note 12, at 830 (arguing the military commitments like NATO can only be effectuated by treaty, and not by way of congressional-executive agreement).

[48] Legislation proposing to limit the usage of sole executive agreements has periodically been introduced, but thus far no bill has been enacted. *See, e.g.,* S.Res. 85, 91st Cong. (1969) (non-binding resolution passed by the Senate expressing its sense that national commitments should be entered pursuant to treaty or executive agreement specifically authorized by Congress); H.R. 4438, 94th Cong. (1976) (proposing to require the President to transmit any agreement involving a national commitment to Congress, and allowing the agreement to take effect only if Congress did not pass a measure disapproving it within 60 days).

---

example, limiting the availability of appropriations to carry out commitments made in a sole executive agreement.[49]

Collective Defense Agreements/"Security Commitments"

The State Department currently lists the United States as being party to seven collective defense agreements, under which members are obligated to assist in the defense of a party to the agreement in the event of an attack upon it: the Inter-American Treaty of Reciprocal Assistance; the North Atlantic Treaty; the Australia, New Zealand, and United States Security Treaty; the Southeast Asian Treaty; and bilateral security treaties with Japan, the Philippines, and South Korea.[50] All seven agreements take the form of treaties that were ratified by the United States between 1947 and 1960.[51] Each agreement, with the exception of the Inter-American Treaty of Reciprocal Assistance (the first to be ratified by the United States), includes a provision specifying that the agreement's requirements are to be carried out in accordance with the parties' respective constitutional processes. These provisions were included to assuage congressional concerns that the agreements could be interpreted as sanctioning the President to engage in military hostilities in defense of treaty parties without further congressional authorization (i.e., a declaration of war or joint resolution authorizing the use of military force).[52]

In addition to these defense treaties, the United States has also adopted security commitments with respect to several former territories and possessions,[53] including pursuant to congressional-executive agreement. Congress has approved compacts changing the status of certain territories to Freely Associated States (FAS), while also imposing upon the United States "the obligation to defend the [FAS] ... from attack or threats thereof as the United States and its citizens are defended."[54] Arguably, these security commitments are distinct from other international defense

---

[49] The Constitution provides that "No money shall be drawn from the Treasury, but in Consequence of Appropriations made by Law." U.S. CONST., art. I, §9, cl. 7.

[50] State Department, Office of the Legal Adviser, *U.S. Collective Defense Arrangements*, at http://www.state.gov/s/l/treaty/collectivedefense/.

[51] Inter-American Treaty of Reciprocal Assistance, 62 Stat. 1681, entered into force December 3, 1948; North Atlantic Treaty, 63 Stat. 2241, entered into force August 24, 1949; Security Treaty Between Australia, New Zealand and the United States of America, 3 U.S.T. 3420, entered into force April 29, 1952; Mutual Defense Treaty Between the United States of America and the Republic of the Philippines, 3 U.S.T. 3947, entered into force August 27, 1952; Mutual Defense Treaty Between the United States of America and the Republic of Korea, 5 U.S.T. 2368, entered into force November 17, 1954; Southeast Asia Collective Defense Treaty, 6 U.S.T. 81, entered into force February 19, 1955; Treaty of Mutual Cooperation and Security Between the United States of America and Japan, 11 U.S.T. 1632, entered into force June 23, 1960 (replacing Security Treaty Between the United States of America and Japan, 3 U.S.T. 3329, entered into force April 28, 1952). In 1954, the United States entered a mutual defense treaty with the Republic of China (Taiwan), 6 U.S.T. 433, but this agreement was terminated by President Carter in 1979.

[52] For background, *see* S.Rept. 797, 90th Cong., at 14-15 (1967) (describing ratification history of North Atlantic Treaty); LOUIS FISHER, PRESIDENTIAL WAR POWER 105-111 (2004) (describing Senate deliberations on North Atlantic Treaty).

[53] For example, the Panama Canal treaties provided that the United States and Panama would, in accordance with their respective constitutional processes, defend the Canal from attack. Treaty Concerning the Permanent Neutrality and Operation of the Panama Canal, with Annexes and Protocol, 33 U.S.T. 1, entered into force October 1, 1979.

[54] Act Approving Compacts of Free Association with the Republic of the Marshall Islands and the Federated States of Micronesia, P.L. 99-239, §311 (1986). *See also* Act approving Compact of Free Association between the United States and the Government of Palau, P.L. 99-658, §352 (1986) (recognizing an attack on Palau as a danger to the United States, and pledging that the United States "would take action to meet the danger to the United States and Palau in accordance with its constitutional processes").

---

arrangements, as they concern commitments to newly sovereign entities over whom the United States formerly exercised extensive and long-standing control.[55]

Consultation Requirements/"Security Arrangements"

The United States also has established security arrangements with other countries in which the United States pledges to take some action in the event that the other country's security is threatened. A 1992 report submitted by President George H. W. Bush to Congress listing U.S. security commitments and arrangements, claimed that unlike "security commitments," which oblige the United States to act in the common defense of a country in case of an armed attack, "security arrangements" generally "oblige the United States to consult with a country in the event of a threat to its security. They may appear in legally binding agreements, such as treaties or executive agreements, or in political documents, such as policy declarations by the President, Secretary of State or Secretary of Defense."[56]

Most legally binding "security arrangements" listed in the President's report constitute sole executive agreements, including agreements with Israel, Egypt, Pakistan, and Liberia.[57] Only one arrangement, committing the United States to the establishment of the Multinational Force and Observers in the Sinai, could clearly be described as a congressional-executive agreement.[58]

Although some scholars and government officials have characterized the terms "security commitment" and "security arrangement" as having distinct and particular meanings, this practice is by no means uniform. Indeed, the question of what constitutes a "security commitment" has long been a subject of dialogue and dispute by the executive and legislative branches.[59]

---

[55] Some have argued that these agreements are "more akin to the Texas and Hawaii annexation resolutions than to international defense arrangements," given the historical status of the FAS. Peter J. Spiro, *Treaties, Executive Agreements, and Constitutional Method*, 79 TEX. L. REV. 961, n. 184 (2001).

[56] TREATIES AND OTHER INTERNATIONAL AGREEMENTS, *supra* note 4, at 248 (quoting A Report on United States Security Arrangements and Commitments with Other Nations, Submitted to the Congress in accordance with Section 1457 of P.L. 101-510, the National Defense Authorization Act of 1991, August 17, 1992).

[57] *Id. See also* Memorandum of Agreement Between the Governments of Israel and the United States Concerning Assurances, Consultations, and United States Policy on Middle East Peace, 32 U.S.T. 2160, entered into force February 27, 1976; Agreement Between the United States and Egypt Concerning Implementation of the Egyptian-Israeli Peace Treaty of March 26, 1979, 32 U.S.T. 2148, entered into force March 26, 1979; Agreement of Cooperation Between the Government of the United States of America and the Government of Pakistan, 10 U.S.T. 317, entered into force May 19, 1959; Agreement of Cooperation Between the Government of the United States of America and the Government of Liberia, 10 U.S.T. 1598, entered into force July 8, 1959.

[58] TREATIES AND OTHER INTERNATIONAL AGREEMENTS, *supra* note 4, at 248. *See also* Multinational Force and Observers Participation Resolution, P.L. 97-132 (1981).

[59] *See* The Proposed U.S. Security Commitment to Iraq: What Will Be In It and Should It Be a Treaty?: Hearing Before the Subcomm. on International Organizations, Human Rights, and Oversight & Subcomm. on the Middle East and South Asia of the House Comm. on Foreign Affairs, January 23, 2008 (statement by Prof. Michael J. Matheson) (recognizing distinction between "security commitment" and "security arrangement," while acknowledging that the "question of what constitutes a 'security commitment' ... has been the subject of dialogue between the executive branch and Congress for decades"). *See also* TREATIES AND OTHER INTERNATIONAL AGREEMENTS, *supra* note 4, at 213-215, 247-250 (discussing legislation considered and enacted by Congress in response to concerns that the Executive had entered agreements imposing national commitments upon the United States without congressional notification or approval).

Other Types of Military Agreements

The United States is also a party to a significant number of defense agreements that do not obligate the United States to take action when another country is attacked, but nonetheless involve military affairs. Categories of such agreements include

- military basing agreements, permitting the United States to build or use permanent facilities, station forces, and conduct certain military activities within a host country;[60]

- access and pre-positioning agreements, permitting the stationing of equipment in a host country and the improvement and use of the country's military or civilian facilities, without establishing a permanent military presence;[61]

- Status of Forces Agreements (SOFAs), defining the legal status of U.S. forces within a host country and typically according them with certain privileges and immunities from the host country's jurisdiction;[62]

- burden-sharing agreements, permitting a host country to assume some of the financial obligations incurred by the stationing of U.S. forces within its territory;[63] and

- agreements providing for arms transfers, military training, and joint military exercises.[64]

Historically, almost all such agreements have taken a form other than treaty. Sometimes these arrangements have taken the form of sole executive agreements; others could be deemed executive agreements pursuant to treaty (e.g., military stationing agreements concluded with other NATO parties); still others have been explicitly or implicitly authorized by statute and may be considered congressional-executive agreements.

As a matter of historical practice, the types of agreements described above have not directly authorized the United States to engage in significant military operations in defense of the host country, though such agreements may supplement separate agreements or U.N. mandates that do.

---

[60] *See, e.g.*, Agreement Between the United States of America and the Kingdom of Greece Concerning Military Facilities, 4 U.S.T. 2189, entered into force October 12, 1953.

[61] An example of such an agreement is the 2005 memorandum of understanding between the United States and Norway, discussed in more detail at American Forces Press Service, *Rumsfeld Signs Pre-positioning Agreement With Norway*, June 8, 2005, at http://www.defenselink.mil/news/newsarticle.aspx?id=16458.

[62] *See, e.g.*, Agreement under Article VI of the Treaty of Mutual Cooperation and Security Regarding Facilities and Areas and the Status of United States Armed Forces in Japan, 11 U.S.T. 1652, entered into force June 23, 1960. The only SOFA agreement to which the United States is a party that was concluded as a treaty is the North Atlantic Treaty Status of Forces Agreement (NATO SOFA), 4 U.S.T. 1792, entered into force August 23, 1953. All supplementary agreements to the NATO SOFA have been executive agreements. For further discussion and background on the use of SOFAs, see CRS Report RL34531, *Status of Forces Agreement (SOFA) What Is It, and How Has It Been Utilized?*, by R. Chuck Mason.

[63] *See, e.g.*, Memorandum of Agreement Between The Ministry of National Defense Republic of Korea and the United States Forces in Korea Regarding The Construction of Facilities at 2nd ID USA To Improve Combined Defense Capabilities, 34 U.S.T. 125, entered into force February 2, 1982.

[64] *See, e.g.*, Agreement for Cooperation on Defense and Economy Between the Governments of the United States of America and of the Republic of Turkey in Accordance with Articles II and III of the North Atlantic Treaty, 32 U.S.T. 3323, entered into force December 18, 1980.

For example, although U.S. basing agreements with Germany, Japan, and South Korea do not expressly authorize the United States to use military force to defend those countries in case of attack, they assist the United States in fulfilling security commitments owed to those countries under separate defense treaties. Arguably, an exception to this practice occurred in 2008, when the United States and Iraq concluded a security agreement, sometimes characterized as a SOFA, which authorized U.S. forces to engage in military operations within Iraq. The agreement is discussed in more detail *infra*.[65]

Agreements Granting the Legal Right to Military Intervention

Besides the categories of agreements described above, the United States has, on occasion, entered into long-term agreements that grant the United States the legal right to intervene militarily within the territory of another party to defend it against internal or external threats. Unlike collective defense agreements, these security agreements provide the United States with the right, but not the duty, to militarily intervene when the security of the other country is threatened. Such agreements may also be distinguished from the authority to intervene recognized under the United Nations Charter. Whereas military intervention agreements discussed below provide the United States with the *positive* legal right to intervene in a country, the U.N. Charter merely provides that its provisions do not "*impair* the inherent right of individual or collective self-defense if an armed attack occurs against a Member of the United Nations, until the Security Council has taken measures necessary to maintain international peace and security."[66]

In the early part of the 20th century, the United States entered into legal agreements with several Latin American countries which granted the United States the right to use military force either to defend those countries from external threat or to preserve domestic tranquility.[67] All of these agreements were concluded as treaties. In 1903, following the Spanish-American War, the United States concluded a treaty with the newly independent Republic of Cuba under which the United States was expressly given "the right to intervene for the preservation of Cuban independence, the maintenance of a government adequate for the protection of life, property, and individual liberty."[68] Similarly, in the aftermath of the U.S. invasion and occupation of Haiti in 1915, a treaty between the two countries was concluded that provided the United States with the right to intervene in Haiti when the United States deemed it necessary.[69] In 1904, the United States ratified a treaty with Panama that provided the United States "the right, at all times and in its discretion" to employ its armed forces for the safety and protection of the Panama Canal and the shipping occurring therein.[70] In 1907, the United States concluded a treaty with the Dominican

---

[65] *See infra* at "Iraq."

[66] Charter of the United Nations, 59 Stat. 1031, entered into force October 24, 1945, art. 51 (italics added).

[67] *See generally* Charles Henry Hyde, 1 International Law: Chiefly As Interpreted and Applied by the United States 27-36 (1922).

[68] Treaty on Relations Between the United States and Cuba, May 22, 1903, 33 Stat. 2248, at art. III. In 1906, acting pursuant to this authority, the United States intervened in Cuba following serious revolutionary activity in order to establish a stable government there.

[69] Treaty on Administration of Haiti: Finances and Development, entered into force November 15, 1915, T.S. 623, 1915 U.S.T. LEXIS 29, at art. XIV (providing that "The high contracting parties shall have authority to take such steps as may be necessary to insure the complete attainment of any of the objects comprehended in this treaty; and, should the necessity occur, the United States will lend an efficient aid for the preservation of Haitian Independence and the maintenance of a government adequate for the protection of life, property and individual liberty.").

[70] Isthmian Canal Convention with the Republic of Panama, entered into force February 26, 1904, 33 Stat. 2234, at art. XXIII. More generally, the agreement provided that the United States "guarantees and will maintain the independence (continued...)

Republic establishing plans for the financial rehabilitation of that country, and authorizing the United States to use military force necessary to effectuate the carrying out of those plans.[71]

There have been numerous instances where a country has permitted or invited the United States to use military force within its territory,[72] but authority to intervene has not been given via treaty. When the Senate initially opted not to approve a treaty authorizing U.S. military and financial involvement in the Dominican Republic, President Theodore Roosevelt entered a temporary *"modus vivendi"* executive agreement adopting similar policies as the unapproved treaty. This agreement, which elicited significant opposition from many Members of Congress as an unconstitutional usurpation of the Senate's treaty power, was terminated following Senate approval of a modified version of the treaty in 1907.[73] Another example of a significant security agreement taking a form other than treaty occurred in 1941 when, prior to the United States entering World War II, President Franklin D. Roosevelt concluded sole executive agreements concerning the stationing of U.S. troops in Iceland and Greenland to protect those territories from attack.[74]

Although publicly available agreements expressly granting the United States the legal right to intervene militarily in another country generally take the form of a treaty, this report does not consider whether any comparable authority is provided pursuant to classified agreements.

Non-Binding Security Arrangements

Some security arrangements are not legally binding; though they may nonetheless carry significant political or moral weight. While executive practice of extending political defense commitments to foreign countries can be traced back to the Monroe Doctrine, in which the United States proclaimed its opposition to further colonization of the Americas by European powers, U.S. pledges to assist foreign states in security matters have become more commonplace in the

---

(...continued)

of Panama." *Id.* at art. I. The agreement also provided the United States with authority to ensure public order in the cities of Panama City and Colon if, in the opinion of the United States, the government of Panama was unable to maintain order. *Id.* at art. VII.

[71] Treaty Between the United States and Dominican Republic Concerning the Collection and Application of Dominican Customs Revenues, proclaimed July 25, 1907, 35 Stat. 1880.

[72] For example, in 1958, President Dwight Eisenhower deployed U.S. troops to Lebanon at the invitation of its government to help protect against a threatened insurrection. Congress had passed legislation in 1957 that authorized such action. *See* P.L. 85-7 (1957). Specifically, the legislation permitted the President to "undertake, in the general area of the Middle East, military assistance programs with any nation or group of nations of that area desiring such assistance." The enactment further provided that "if the President determines the necessity thereof, the United States is prepared to use armed forces to assist any such nation or group of such nations requesting assistance against armed aggression from any country controlled by international communism: *Provided*, that such employment shall be consonant with the treaty obligations of the United States and with the Constitution of the United States."

[73] For further discussion, see W. Stull Holt, TREATIES DEFEATED BY THE SENATE 212-229 (1933) (discussing events leading to the ratification of the 1907 treaty with the Dominican Republic). In his autobiography, Roosevelt suggested that a treaty was preferable to the executive agreement he entered with the Dominican Republic, because "a treaty ... was the law of the land and not merely ... a direction of the Chief Executive which would lapse when that particular executive left office." ACKERMAN & GOLOVE, *supra* note 13, at 819 (italics omitted) (quoting THEODORE ROOSEVELT, AN AUTOBIOGRAPHY 510 (1920)).

[74] Agreement Between the United States and Denmark Concerning the Defense of Greenland, signed April 9, 1941, 55 Stat. 1245; Agreement Concerning Defense of Iceland By United States Forces, July 1, 1941, 55 Stat. 1547.

---

post-World War II era. Such commitments may take several forms, including a unilateral pledge or policy statement by the executive or a joint declaration between U.S. and foreign officials.

For example, bilateral arrangements authorizing U.S. military intervention, when not concluded as treaties, generally have not taken the form of a legally binding, permanent agreement.[75] Instead, in non-treaty arrangements authorizing U.S. intervention, the host country often retains full discretion as to the degree and duration of U.S. presence within its territory. In 1962, for instance, U.S. Secretary of State Dean Rusk and Thai Foreign Minister Thanat Khoman issued a joint declaration in which Secretary Rusk expressed "the firm intention of the United States to aid Thailand, its ally and historic friend, in resisting Communist aggression and subversion."[76] The United States thereafter deployed armed forces to Thailand to assist the government in combating communist forces.

The executive's authority to enter such arrangements, and, more broadly, to engage in military operations in other countries without congressional approval, has been the subject of long-standing dispute between Congress and the executive.[77] In 1969, the Senate passed the National Commitments Resolution, stating the sense of the Senate that "a national commitment by the United States results only from affirmative action taken by the executive and legislative branches of the United States government by means of a treaty [or legislative enactment] ... specifically providing for such commitment."[78] The Resolution defined a "national commitment" as including "the use of the armed forces of the United States on foreign territory, or a promise to assist a foreign country ... by the use of armed forces ... either immediately or upon the happening of certain events."[79]

According to the committee report accompanying the Resolution, the motivation for the Resolution was concern over the growing development of "constitutional imbalance" in matters of foreign relations, with Presidents frequently making significant foreign commitments on behalf

---

[75] *See supra* note 72 (discussing U.S. intervention in Lebanon in 1958).

[76] For text of the joint declaration, see Dept. of State, American Foreign Policy: Current Documents, 1962, pp. 1091-1093.

[77] *See* S.Rept. 91-129 (1969) (Senate Committee on Foreign Relations report in favor of the National Commitments Resolution, S.Res. 85, criticizing the undertaking of "national commitments" by the Executive, either through international agreements or unilateral pledges to other countries, without congressional involvement) [hereinafter "Committee Report"]. The vast majority of U.S. military interventions in other countries have been to protect U.S. persons, property, or interests. *See* CRS Report R41677, *Instances of Use of United States Armed Forces Abroad, 1798-2010*, by Richard F. Grimmett. The Executive has historically claimed broad authority to deploy armed forces to protect these interests, even in the absence of clear congressional authorization. *See, e.g.,* Dept. of Justice, Office of Legal Counsel (OLC), *Authority to Use Military Force in Libya*, 2011 OLC LEXIS 1, at 8 (2011) (claiming that "prolonged and substantial military engagements, typically involving exposure of U.S. military personnel to significant risk over a substantial period" may generally require prior congressional authorization, but "historical practice of presidential military action without congressional approval precludes any suggestion that Congress's authority to declare war covers every military engagement, however limited, that the President initiates"); OLC, 4A U.S. Op. Off. Legal Counsel 185, *Presidential Power to Use the Armed Forces Abroad Without Statutory Authorization* (1980) (alleging presidential authority to deploy forces to protect, and retaliate for injuries suffered by U.S. persons and property); OLC, *The President's Constitutional Authority To Conduct Military Operations Against Terrorists And Nations Supporting Them*, 2001 OLC LEXIS 14 (2001) (asserting presidential authority, even in the absence of congressional action, to take military action against entities responsible for the 9/11 terrorist attacks, as well authority to preemptively use force against entities that "pose a similar threat to the security of the United States and the lives of its people, whether at home or overseas").

[78] S.Res. 85, 91st Congress, 1st Sess. (1969).

[79] *Id.*

---

of the United States without congressional action. Among other things, the report criticized a practice it described as "commitment by accretion," by which a

> sense of binding commitment arises out of a series of executive declarations, no one of which in itself would be thought of as constituting a binding obligation. Simply repeating something often enough with regard to our relations with some particular country, we come to support that our honor is involved in an engagement no less solemn than a duly ratified treaty.[80]

The National Commitments Resolution took the form of a sense of the Senate resolution, and accordingly had no legal effect. Although Congress has occasionally considered legislation that would bar the adoption of significant military commitments without congressional action,[81] no such measure has been enacted. The executive branch regularly makes unilateral security pledges or enters non-binding arrangements with foreign countries concerning security matters.[82] The primary means Congress uses to exercise oversight authority over such non-binding arrangements is its appropriations power, by which it may limit or condition actions the United States may take in furtherance of the arrangement.

Examples of Bilateral Security Agreements

The following sections discuss in greater detail the form, nature, and content of bilateral security agreements made by the United States with Afghanistan, Germany, Japan, South Korea, the Philippines, and Iraq.

Afghanistan

Following the terrorist attacks of September 11, 2001, the United States initiated Operation Enduring Freedom to combat Al Qaeda and prevent the Taliban regime in Afghanistan from providing them with safe harbor. Shortly thereafter, the Taliban regime was ousted by U.S. and allied forces, and the United States thereafter concluded a number of security agreements with the new Afghan government. In 2002, the United States and Afghanistan, by an exchange of notes,[83] entered into an agreement regarding economic grants under the Foreign Assistance Act of 1961,[84] as amended. Additionally, the agreement allows for the furnishing of defense articles, defense

---

[80] Committee Report, *supra* note 77, at 26.

[81] *See, e.g.,* H.R. 4438, Executive Agreements Review Act, 94th Cong., 1st Sess. (proposing to establish legislative veto over executive agreements involving national commitments); S.Res. 24, Treaty Powers Resolution, 95th Cong., 1st Sess. (proposing that it would not be in order for the Senate to consider any legislation authorizing funds to implement any international agreement which the Senate has found to constitute a treaty, unless the Senate has given its advice and consent to treaty ratification).

[82] *See generally* The November 26 Declaration of Principles: Implications for UN Resolutions on Iraq and for Congressional Oversight: Hearing of the Subcommittee on International Organizations, Human Rights, and Oversight, February 8, 2008 (statement of Prof. Michael J. Glennon discussing presidential practice of entering non-binding security arrangements).

[83] Agreement Regarding Grants under the Foreign Assistance Act of 1961,U.S.-Afghanistan, T.I.A.S. No. 02-413, entered into force April 13, 2002, available at http://www.state.gov/documents/organization/165174.pdf.

[84] P.L. 87-195, 75 Stat. 424 (September 4 1961). The Foreign Assistance Act of 1961, as amended, and related legislation provide statutory authority for a broad range of executive agreements in matters including security and economic cooperation, and appear to serve as a legal authority supporting a substantial number of executive agreements entered into in recent decades.

---

services, and related training, pursuant to the United States International Military and Education Training Program (IMET),[85] from the U.S. government to the Afghanistan Interim Administration (AIA).

An agreement exists regarding the status of military and civilian personnel of the U.S. Department of Defense present in Afghanistan in connection with cooperative efforts in response to terrorism, humanitarian and civic assistance, military training and exercises, and other activities.[86] Such personnel are to be accorded "a status equivalent to that accorded to the administrative and technical staff" of the U.S. Embassy under the Vienna Convention on Diplomatic Relations of 1961.[87] Accordingly, U.S. personnel are immune from criminal prosecution by Afghan authorities, and are immune from civil and administrative jurisdiction except with respect to acts performed outside the course of their duties.[88] In the agreement, the Islamic Transitional Government of Afghanistan (ITGA)[89] explicitly authorizes the U.S. government to exercise criminal jurisdiction over U.S. personnel, and the government of Afghanistan is not permitted to surrender U.S. personnel to the custody of another state, international tribunal, or any other entity without consent of the U.S. government. Although the agreement was signed by the ITGA, the subsequently elected government of the Islamic Republic of Afghanistan assumed responsibility for ITGA's legal obligations, and the agreement remains in force. The agreement does not appear to provide immunity for contract personnel.

The agreement with Afghanistan does not expressly authorize the United States to carry out military operations within Afghanistan, but it recognizes that such operations are "ongoing." Congress authorized the use of military force there (and elsewhere) by joint resolution in 2001, for targeting "those nations, organizations, or persons [who] planned, authorized, committed, or aided the terrorist attacks that occurred on September 11, 2001."[90] The U.N. Security Council implicitly recognized that the use of force was appropriate in response to the September 11, 2001, terrorist attacks,[91] and subsequently authorized the deployment of an International Security Assistance Force (ISAF) to Afghanistan.[92] Subsequent U.N. Security Council resolutions provide a continuing mandate for ISAF,[93] calling upon it to "work in close consultation with" Operation

---

[85] 22 U.S.C. §2347 *et seq.*

[86] Agreement Regarding the Status of United States Military and Civilian Personnel of the U.S. Department of Defense Present in Afghanistan, T.I.A.S., 2002 U.S.T. LEXIS 100, entered into force May 28, 2003 [hereinafter "U.S.-Afghan SOFA"].

[87] *Id.*

[88] Vienna Convention on Diplomatic Relations of April 18, 1961, T.I.A.S. 7502; 23 U.S.T. 3227.

[89] The transitional government has since been replaced by the fully elected Government of the Islamic Republic of Afghanistan. For information about the political development of Afghanistan since 2001, see CRS Report RS21922, *Afghanistan Politics, Elections, and Government Performance*, by Kenneth Katzman.

[90] P.L. 107-40 (September 18, 2001); 115 Stat. 224.

[91] U.N.S.C. Res. 1368 (September 12, 2001) ("Recognizing the inherent right of individual or collective self-defence in accordance with the [UN] Charter," and expressing its "readiness to take all necessary steps to respond to the terrorist attacks").

[92] U.N.S.C. Res. 1386 (December 20, 2001).

[93] ISAF has its own status of forces agreement with the Afghan government in the form of an annex to a Military Technical Agreement entitled "Arrangements Regarding the Status of the International Security Assistance Force." The agreement provides that all ISAF and supporting personnel are subject to the exclusive jurisdiction of their respective national elements for criminal or disciplinary matters, and that such personnel are immune from arrest or detention by Afghan authorities and may not be turned over to any international tribunal or any other entity or State without the express consent of the contributing nation. In 2003, NATO assumed command of ISAF in Afghanistan.

Enduring Freedom (OEF—the U.S.-led coalition conducting military operations in Afghanistan) in carrying out the mandate.[94] While there is no explicit U.N. mandate authorizing the OEF, Security Council resolutions appear to provide ample recognition of the legitimacy of its operations, most recently by calling upon the Afghan government, "with the assistance of the international community, including the International Security Assistance Force and Operation Enduring Freedom coalition, in accordance with their respective designated responsibilities as they evolve, to continue to address the threat to the security and stability of Afghanistan posed by the Taliban, Al-Qaida, other extremist groups and criminal activities."[95]

In 2004, the United States and Afghanistan entered an acquisition and cross-servicing agreement, with annexes.[96] An acquisition and cross-servicing agreement (ACSA) is an agreement providing logistic support, supplies, and services to foreign militaries on a cash-reimbursement, replacement-in-kind, or exchange of equal value basis.[97] After consultation with the Secretary of State, the Secretary of Defense is authorized to enter into an ACSA with a government of a NATO country, a subsidiary body of NATO, or the United Nations Organization or any regional international organization of which the United States is a member.[98] Additionally, the Secretary of Defense may enter into an ACSA with a country not included in the above categories, if after consultation with the Secretary of State, a determination is made that it is in the best interests of the national security of the United States.[99] If the country is not a member of NATO, the Secretary of Defense must submit notice, at least 30 days prior to designation, to the Committee on Armed Services and the Committee on Foreign Relations of the Senate and the Committee on Armed Services and the Committee on Foreign Affairs of the House of Representatives.[100]

Since at least 2003, the United States has entered into several accommodation assignment agreements with Afghanistan regarding the use of land and facilities, including for the internment of captured enemy forces.[101] Beginning in late 2001, the United States and its coalition partners utilized the Bagram Airfield for military purposes in the conflict against the Taliban and Al Qaeda. The Bagram Airfield also served as the primary facility used to detain suspected enemy belligerents captured in the conflict until 2010,[102] when a new detention facility was completed in Parwan, Afghanistan.[103] The detention center had reportedly been slated to be turned over to Afghan authority by January 2012, but rapid growth of the prisoner population caused the transfer to be delayed.[104] In March 2012, the United States and the Afghan government concluded an

---

[94] *See* U.N.S.C. Res. 1776 §5 (September 19, 2007); U.N.S.C. Res. 1707 §4 (2007).

[95] U.N.S.C. Res. 1746 §25 (2007). For additional information on the war in Afghanistan, see CRS Report R40156, *War in Afghanistan Strategy, Operations, and Issues for Congress*, by Catherine Dale.

[96] Acquisition and Cross-servicing Agreement, with Annexes, U.S.-Afghanistan, T.I.A.S. No. 04-216, entered into force February 16, 2004, available at http://www.state.gov/documents/organization/173052.pdf.

[97] 10 U.S.C. §§2341-2350.

[98] *Id.* at §2342(a)(1).

[99] *Id.* at §2342(b)(1).

[100] *Id.* at §2342(b)(2).

[101] Declaration of Colonel James W. Gray, filed March 5, 2007, Al Maqaleh v. Gates, 06-CV-01669 (U.S. D.D.C.), available at http://graphics8.nytimes.com/packages/pdf/topics/bagram/Affidavit.pdf [hereinafter "Gray Declaration"].

[102] Detainees were held in the Bagram Theater Internment Facility within the Airfield.

[103] *See* Lisa Daniel, "Task Force Ensures Fair Detainee Treatment, Commander Says," *American Forces Press Service*, August 6, 2010, available at http://www.defense.gov/News/NewsArticle.aspx?ID=103004.

[104] *See* Kevin Sieff, "Afghan Prison Transfer Delayed," *Washington Post*, August 12, 2011, available at http://www.washingtonpost.com/world/asia-pacific/afghan-prison-transfer-delayed/2011/08/12/gIQApCGMBJ_story.html.

agreement effectuating the transfer of the Parwan detention facility to Afghan control.[105] The memorandum also contemplates U.S. forces maintaining continued control of Parwan detainees during a six-month handover period, at which point all Afghan nationals in U.S. custody shall be transferred to the control of Afghanistan.

A separate memorandum of understanding was also concluded in April 2012 concerning special operations (night raids) on Afghan soil. Under the agreement, the parties affirm that such operations will be "conducted by Afghan Forces with support of U.S. Forces in accordance with Afghan laws."[106] Afghan forces are designated with responsibility for the "temporary holding" of persons captured in the course of such operations. Afghan citizens detained by U.S. forces outside of special operations are to be transferred to Afghan authorities or released.

On May 2, 2012, U.S. President Barack Obama and Afghan President Hamid Karzai signed the Enduring Strategic Partnership Agreement Between the United States of America and the Islamic Republic of Afghanistan (Strategic Partnership Agreement).[107] The Strategic Partnership Agreement is a legally binding agreement under which the parties pledge to work cooperatively in a number of fields, including on promoting shared democratic values, advancing long-term security, reinforcing regional security, social and economic development, and strengthening Afghan institutions and governance. The agreement remains in force until the end of 2024, unless terminated at an earlier date by either party.

In the area of security, the Strategic Partnership Agreement provides that the United States and Afghanistan shall "initiate negotiations on a Bilateral Security Agreement … with the goal of concluding within one year" an agreement to replace the current agreement relating to the status of military and civilian personnel currently in Afghanistan.[108] The Strategic Partnership Agreement also states that Afghanistan "shall provide U.S. forces continued access to and use of Afghan facilities through 2014, and beyond as may be agreed in the Bilateral Security Agreement" and that the United States "reaffirms that it does not see permanent military facilities in Afghanistan, or a presence that is a threat to Afghanistan's neighbors." Additionally, the Agreement determines that the "nature and scope of the future presence and operations of U.S. forces in Afghanistan" shall be addressed in the Bilateral Security Agreement to be negotiated.

---

[105] Memorandum of Understanding between the Islamic Republic of Afghanistan and the United States of America on Transfer of U.S. Detention Facilities in Afghan Territory to Afghanistan, signed March 9, 2012, available at http://www.lawfareblog.com/wp-content/uploads/2012/04/2012-03-09-Signed-MOU-on-Detentions-Transfer-2.pdf.

[106] Memorandum of Understanding between the Islamic Republic of Afghanistan and the United States of America on Afghanization of Special Operations on Afghan Soil, signed April 8, 2012, available at http://www.isaf.nato.int/images/20120408_01_memo.pdf.

[107] The text of this agreement is available at http://www.whitehouse.gov/sites/default/files/2012.06.01u.s.-afghanistanspasignedtext.pdf [hereinafter "Strategic Partnership Agreement"].

[108] U.S.-Afghan SOFA, *supra* note 86.

Iraq[109]

In 2007, following the removal of the Saddam Hussein regime from power, the United States and the post-Saddam government of Iraq signed a Declaration of Principles for a Long-Term Relationship of Cooperation and Friendship Between the Republic of Iraq and the United States of America.[110] The Declaration announced the intention of the parties to negotiate a long-term security agreement that would have committed the United States to provide security assurances to Iraq and maintain a long-term military presence in that country. This announcement became a source of congressional interest, in part because of statements by Administration officials that such an agreement would not be submitted to the legislative branch for approval.[111] Congressional concern dissipated when U.S.-Iraq negotiations culminated in the signing of two separate agreements on November 17, 2008, neither of which provided for a long-term security commitment by the United States:[112] (1) the Strategic Framework Agreement for a Relationship of Friendship and Cooperation between the United States and the Republic of Iraq (Strategic Framework Agreement),[113] and (2) the Agreement Between the United States of America and Republic of Iraq On the Withdrawal of United States Forces from Iraq and the Organization of Their Activities during Their Temporary Presence in Iraq (Security Agreement).[114] Indeed, rather than establishing a long-term security commitment by the United States, the Security Agreement concluded by the parties instead called for the withdrawal of U.S. forces from Iraq within three years.

The concluded agreements cover different issues and were intended by the parties to have different legal significance. The Strategic Framework Agreement, which remains in force, is a legally binding agreement under which the parties pledge to work cooperatively in a number of fields, including on diplomatic, security, economic, cultural, and law enforcement matters. In the area of security, the Agreement provides that the United States and Iraq shall "continue to foster close cooperation concerning defense and security arrangements," which are to be undertaken

---

[109] In the 1950s, almost 40 years prior to the 1991 Persian Gulf War, the United States entered into a series of agreements with Iraq, including (1) a military assistance agreement (T.I.A.S. 3108. Agreement of April 21, 1954); (2) an agreement relating to the disposition of military equipment and materials provided under the military assistance agreement (T.I.A.S. 3289. Agreement of July 25, 1955); and (3) an economic assistance agreement (T.I.A.S. 3835. Agreement of May 18 and 22, 1957). However, in response to the Revolution of July 14, 1958 and the subsequent change in the government of Iraq, the United States agreed to a termination of the above agreements (10 U.S.T. 1415; T.I.A.S. 4289; 357 U.N.T.S. 153. Exchange of notes at Baghdad May 30 and July 7, 1959. Entered into force July 21, 1959).

[110] The text of this agreement is available at http://georgewbush-whitehouse.archives.gov/news/releases/2007/11/20071126-11.html [hereinafter "Declaration of Principles"]. For a historical perspective of U.S. operations in Iraq and issues related to Iraqi governance and security, see CRS Report RL31339, *Iraq Post-Saddam Governance and Security*, by Kenneth Katzman, and CRS Report RL33793, *Iraq Regional Perspectives and U.S. Policy*, by Christopher M. Blanchard et al.

[111] For further discussion, see CRS Report RL34568, *U.S.-Iraq Agreements Congressional Oversight Activities and Legislative Response*, by Matthew C. Weed.

[112] Prior to concluding the agreements, the United States entered into numerous defense-related agreements with the Interim Government of Iraq, including an agreement regarding grants under the Foreign Assistance Act of 1961, or successor legislation, and other items provided to the government of Iraq.

[113] Strategic Framework Agreement for a Relationship of Friendship and Cooperation between the United States of America and the Republic of Iraq, T.I.A.S., 2008 U.S.T. LEXIS 116. Signed in Baghdad November 17, 2008. Entered into force January 1, 2009.

[114] Withdrawal of United States Forces from Iraq and the Organization of Their Activities during Their Temporary Presence in Iraq, T.I.A.S. 2008 U.S.T. LEXIS 115. Signed in Baghdad November 17, 2008. Entered into force January 1, 2009.

---

pursuant to the terms of the Security Agreement.[115] The Strategic Framework Agreement also states that "the temporary presence of U.S. forces in Iraq [was] at the request and invitation of the sovereign government of Iraq," and that the United States could not "use Iraqi land, sea, or air as a launching or transit point for attacks against other countries[,] nor seek or request permanent bases or a permanent military presence in Iraq."

The Security Agreement remained in effect for three years, and contained provisions addressing a variety of military matters, including a deadline for the withdrawal of all U.S. forces from Iraq by December 31, 2011. The Agreement also contained numerous provisions resembling those regularly contained in SOFAs concluded by the United States.[116] Specifically, the Agreement contained provisions concerning the parties' right to assert civil and criminal jurisdiction over U.S. forces, as well as provisions which establish rules and procedures applicable to U.S. forces relating to the carrying of weapons, the wearing of uniforms, entry and exit into Iraq, taxes, customs, and claims. The Security Agreement established other rules and requirements traditionally not found in SOFAs concluded by the United States, including provisions addressing combat operations by U.S. forces.

The Security and Strategic Framework Agreements entered into force on January 1, 2009, following an exchange of diplomatic notes between the United States and Iraq. Although the agreements required approval on multiple levels by the Iraqi government, the Bush Administration did not submit the agreements to the Senate for its advice and consent as a treaty or request statutory authorization for the agreements by Congress.

There has been some controversy regarding whether these agreements were properly entered on behalf of the United States by the executive without the participation of Congress.[117] As previously discussed, security agreements authorizing the United States to take military action in defense of another country have typically been ratified as treaties.[118] It could be argued that the Security Agreement, which contemplated the United States engaging in military operations in Iraq and potentially defending the Iraqi government from external or internal security threats, properly required congressional authorization for it to be legally binding under U.S. law. On the other hand, because Congress had authorized the President to engage in military operations in Iraq, both pursuant to the 2002 Authorization to Use Military Force Against Iraq and subsequent appropriations measures in effect for the duration of the Security Agreement, it arguably had

---

[115] Initially, the Bush Administration expected any negotiated strategic framework agreement with Iraq to take the form of a political, rather than a legally binding agreement. *Hearing of the Subcommittee on the Middle East and South Asia, and the Subcommittee on International Organizations, Human Rights, and Oversight of the House Foreign Affairs Committee; Declaration and Principles Future U.S. Commitments to Iraq*, March 4, 2008 (statement by Ambassador David M. Satterfield in response to question by Representative William Delahunt). Subsequent developments, including pressure from the Iraqi parliament that the negotiated U.S.-Iraq security agreements be submitted to it for approval before they could go into effect for Iraq, resulted in the agreements taking the form of legally binding instruments. *See also* STATE DEPT, TREATIES IN FORCE, A LIST OF TREATIES AND OTHER INTERNATIONAL AGREEMENTS OF THE UNITED STATES IN FORCE (2011) (listing both the U.S.-Iraq Security and Strategic Framework Agreements as legal agreements).

[116] For further discussion, see CRS Report R40011, *U.S.-Iraq Withdrawal/Status of Forces Agreement Issues for Congressional Oversight*, by R. Chuck Mason.

[117] *See* CRS Report RL34568, *U.S.-Iraq Agreements Congressional Oversight Activities and Legislative Response*, by Matthew C. Weed (discussing congressional hearings and proposed legislation addressing the U.S.-Iraq security arrangement).

[118] *See supra* at "Collective Defense Agreements/"Security Commitments""""

---

impliedly authorized the President to enter short-term agreements with Iraq in order to facilitate these operations.[119]

Germany

In 1951, the United States and Germany entered into an agreement[120] related to the assurances required under the Mutual Security Act of 1951.[121] This act is "an act to maintain the security and promote the foreign policy and provide for the general welfare of the United States by furnishing [material] assistance to friendly nations in the interest of international peace and security."[122] Specifically, the agreement references the "statement of purpose contained in Section 2 of the Mutual Security Act of 1951, and reaffirms that ... [Germany] is firmly committed to join in promoting international understanding and good will and in maintaining world peace and to take such action as may be mutually agreed upon to eliminate causes of international tension."[123] The statement of purpose in Section 2 of the act is

> to maintain the security and to promote the foreign policy of the United States by authorizing military, economic, and technical assistance to friendly countries to strengthen the mutual security and individual and collective defense of the free world, to develop their resources in the interest of their security and independence and the national interest of the United States and to facilitate the effective participation of those countries in the United Nations system for collective security.[124]

In 1955, the United States and Germany, both parties to the North Atlantic Treaty, entered into an agreement on mutual defense assistance,[125] obligating the United States to provide for "such equipment, materials, services, or other assistance as may be agreed" to Germany.[126] The agreement reflected the

> desire to foster international peace and security through measures which further the ability of nations dedicated to the purposes and principles of the Charter of the United Nations to participate effectively in arrangements for collective self-defense in support of those purposes and principles, and conscious of the determination to give their full cooperation to United Nations collective security arrangements and measures and efforts to obtain agreement on universal regulation of armaments under adequate guarantees against violation

---

[119] The 2002 Authorization to Use Military Force Against Iraq (2002 AUMF, P.L. 107-243) authorized the President to use military force as he deemed necessary and appropriate to "(1)defend the national security of the United States against the continuing threat posed by Iraq; and (2) enforce all relevant United Nations Security Council resolutions regarding Iraq." It could be argued that the removal of Saddam Hussein's regime from power in Iraq and the termination of the U.N. Security Council mandate mean that the 2002 AUMF no longer serves as a legal basis for U.S. operations in Iraq. Regardless of the continuing viability of the 2002 AUMF, Congress's appropriation of funds in support of ongoing military operations may be viewed as legal authorization for those operations. For further discussion, see CRS Report RL33837, *Congressional Authority to Limit U.S. Military Operations in Iraq, supra* note 34.

[120] 3 U.S.T. 4564; T.I.A.S. 2607; 181 U.N.T.S. 45. Exchange of letters at Bonn December 19 and 28, 1951.

[121] P.L. 82-165, 65 Stat. 373 (October 10, 1951).

[122] *Id.*

[123] 3 U.S.T. 4564; T.I.A.S. 2607; 181 U.N.T.S. 45.

[124] 65 Stat. 373.

[125] 6 U.S.T. 5999; T.I.A.S. 3443; 240 U.N.T.S. 47. Signed at Bonn June 30, 1955. Entered into force December 27, 1955.

[126] *Id.*

or evasion; [and] considering the support which the Government of the United States of America has brought to these principles by enacting the Mutual Security Act of 1954,[127] which authorizes the furnishing of military assistance to certain nations[.][128]

Germany guarantees that it "will not use such assistance for any act inconsistent with the strictly defensive character of the North Atlantic Treaty, or, without the prior consent of the [United States], for any other purpose."[129] The mutual defense assistance agreement is the basis for numerous subsequent agreements between the United States and Germany.[130]

In 1959, the countries entered into an agreement implementing the NATO SOFA of 1953.[131] The agreement provided additional supplemental agreements, beyond those contained in the NATO SOFA, specific to the relationship between the United States and Germany.

Japan

In 1954, the United States and Japan entered into a mutual defense assistance agreement with annexes.[132] The agreement was amended on April 18 and June 23, 2006. The agreement references the Treaty of Peace signed between the countries in San Francisco, CA, in 1951.[133] The Mutual Defense Assistance Act of 1949[134] and the Mutual Security Act of 1951[135] are also referenced in the agreement as they provide for the furnishing of defense assistance by the United States.[136] The agreement provides that the United States and Japan "will make available to the other and to such other governments as the two Governments signatory to the present Agreement may in each case agree upon, such equipment, materials, services, or other assistance as the Government furnishing such assistance may authorize" subject to the conditions and provisions of the Mutual Defense Assistance Act of 1949, the Mutual Security Act of 1951, and appropriation acts which may affect the furnishing of assistance.[137]

In 1960, the countries entered into the Treaty of Mutual Cooperation and Security Between the United States of America and Japan.[138] The treaty was amended on December 26, 1990.[139] Article

---

[127] P.L. 83-665, 68 Stat. 832 (August 26, 1954).

[128] 6 U.S.T. 5999; T.I.A.S. 3443; 240 U.N.T.S. 47.

[129] *Id.*

[130] *See, e.g.,* Mutual Defense Assistance: Disposition of Military Equipment and Materials. 6 U.S.T. 6005; T.I.A.S. 3444; 240 U.N.T.S. 69. Exchange of notes at Bonn June 30, 1955. Entered into force December 27, 1955. Mutual Defense Assistance: Purchase of Certain Military Equipment, Materials, and Services. 7 U.S.T. 2787; T.I.A.S. 3660; 278 U.N.T.S. 9. Exchange of notes at Washington October 8, 1956. Entered into force December 12, 1956. Defense: Training of German Army Personnel. 8 U.S.T. 149; T.I.A.S. 3753; 280 U.N.T.S. 63. Exchange of notes at Bonn December 12, 1956. Entered into force December 12, 1956.

[131] 14 U.S.T. 689; T.I.A.S. 5352; 490 U.N.T.S. 30. Signed at Bonn August 3, 1959. Entered into force July 1, 1963.

[132] 5 U.S.T. 661; T.I.A.S. 2957; 232 U.N.T.S. 169. Signed at Tokyo March 8, 1954. Entered into force May 1, 1954.

[133] 3 U.S.T. 3169; T.I.A.S. 2490. Signed at San Francisco September, 8, 1951. Entered into force April 28, 1952.

[134] 63 Stat. 714.

[135] 65 Stat. 373.

[136] 5 U.S.T. 661; T.I.A.S. 2957; 232 U.N.T.S. 169.

[137] *Id.*

[138] 11 U.S.T. 1632; T.I.A.S. 4509; 373 U.N.T.S. 186. Signed at Washington January 19, 1960. Entered into force June 23, 1960.

[139] T.I.A.S. 12335.

III of the Treaty provides that the countries, "individually and in cooperation with each other, by means of continuous and effective self-help and mutual aid will maintain and develop, subject to their constitutional provisions, their capacities to resist armed attack."[140] Article V provides that the countries recognize "that an armed attack against either party in the territories under the administration of Japan would be dangerous to its own peace and safety and declares that it would act to meet the common danger in accordance with its constitutional provisions and processes."[141] Under Article VI of the Treaty, the United States is granted "the use by its land, air and naval forces of facilities and areas in Japan" in order to contribute "to the security of Japan and maintenance of international peace and security in the Far East[.]"[142] Article VI provides further that the use of facilities and the status of U.S. Armed Forces will be governed under a separate agreement.[143]

Under Article VI of the Treaty of Mutual Cooperation and Security Between the United States of America and Japan, the countries entered into a SOFA in 1960.[144] The SOFA addresses the use of facilities by the U.S. Armed Forces, as well as the status of U.S. forces in Japan. The agreement has been modified at least four times since the original agreement.[145]

South Korea

In 1948, the United States and South Korea entered into an agreement related to the transfer of authority to the government of South Korea and the withdrawal of U.S. occupation forces.[146] Shortly after the initial agreement, the United States and Korea entered into a second agreement concerning interim military and security matters during a transitional period.[147] This executive agreement was between the President of the Republic of Korea and the Commanding General, U.S. Army Forces in Korea.[148] The agreement calls for the "Commanding General, United States Army Forces in Korea, pursuant to directives from his government and within his capabilities" to "organize, train and equip the Security forces of the Republic of Korea" with the obligation to train and equip ceasing "upon the completion of withdrawal from Korea of forces under his command."[149] The agreement also requires the Commanding General, U.S. Army Forces in Korea, to retain authority to exercise over-all operational control of security forces of Korea until withdrawal, as contemplated by Resolution No. II passed by the United Nations General Assembly on November 14, 1948.[150]

---

[140] 11 U.S.T. 1632; T.I.A.S. 4509; 373 U.N.T.S. 186.

[141] *Id.*

[142] *Id.*

[143] *Id.*

[144] 11 U.S.T. 1652; T.I.A.S. 4510; 373 U.N.T.S. 248. Signed at Washington January 19, 1960. Entered into force June 23, 1960.

[145] Agreements concerning new special measures relating to Article XXIV (related to costs of maintenance of U.S. forces in Japan and furnishment of rights of way related to facilities used by U.S. forces in Japan) of the agreement of January 19, 1960, have been signed in 1991, 1995, 2000, and 2006.

[146] Exchange of letters at Seoul August 9 and 11, 1948. Entered into force August 11, 1948.

[147] 62 Stat. 3817; T.I.A.S. 1918; 9 Bevans 477; 79 U.N.T.S. 57. Signed at Seoul August 24, 1948. Entered into force August 24, 1948.

[148] *Id.*

[149] 62 Stat. 3818.

[150] *Id.*

Article III of the Agreement contains provisions related to the status of U.S. forces during the transition period. The Commanding General, U.S. Army Forces in Korea, "shall retain exclusive jurisdiction over the personnel of his command, both military and civilian, including their dependents, whose conduct as individuals shall be in keeping with pertinent laws of the Republic of Korea."[151] The agreement provides that any individuals under the jurisdiction of the Commanding General who are apprehended by law enforcement agencies of South Korea shall be immediately turned over to the custody and control of the Commanding General. Individuals not under jurisdiction of the Commanding General, but apprehended in acts detrimental to the security of personnel or property under his jurisdiction, shall be turned over to the custody and control of the government of South Korea.[152]

In 1950, the countries entered into a mutual defense assistance agreement.[153] The mutual defense agreement references the Military Defense Act of 1949,[154] which provides for the furnishing of military assistance by the United States to South Korea. The mutual defense assistance agreement provides that each country "will make or continue to make available to the other, and to other Governments, such equipment, materials, services, or other military assistance" in support of economic recovery that is essential to international peace and security.[155]

The United States and South Korea entered into a mutual security agreement in 1952.[156] The mutual security agreement references the Mutual Security Act of 1951,[157] which provides for military, economic, and technical assistance in order to strengthen the mutual security of the free world. The mutual security agreement provides that South Korea agrees to promote international understanding and good will and to take action, that is mutually agreed upon, to eliminate causes of international tensions.[158]

In 1954, the countries entered into a mutual defense treaty.[159] As part of the treaty the countries agree to attempt to settle international disputes peacefully, consult whenever the political independence or security of either party is threatened by external armed attack, and that either party would act to meet the common danger in accordance with their respective constitutional processes.[160] Article IV of the treaty grants the United States "the right to dispose ... land, air and sea forces in and about the territory" of South Korea.[161] Pursuant to the treaty, specifically Article IV, in 1966, the countries entered into a SOFA with agreed minutes and an exchange of notes.[162] It was subsequently amended January 18, 2001.

---

[151] *Id.* at 3819.

[152] *Id.*

[153] 1 U.S.T. 137; T.I.A.S. 2019; 80 U.N.T.S. 205. Signed at Seoul January 26, 1950. Entered into force January 26, 1950.

[154] P.L. 81-329, 63 Stat. 714 (October 6, 1949).

[155] 1 U.S.T. 137; T.I.A.S. 2019; 80 U.N.T.S. 205.

[156] 3 U.S.T. 4619; T.I.A.S. 2612; 179 U.N.T.S. 105. Exchange of notes at Pusan January 4 and 7, 1952. Entered into force January 7, 1952.

[157] P.L. 82-165, 65 Stat. 373 (October 10, 1951).

[158] 3 U.S.T. 4619; T.I.A.S. 2612; 179 U.N.T.S. 105.

[159] 5 U.S.T. 2368; T.I.A.S. 3097; 238 U.N.T.S. 199. Signed at Washington October 1, 1953. Entered into force November 17, 1954.

[160] *Id.*

[161] *Id.*

[162] 17 U.S.T. 1677; T.I.A.S. 6127; 674 U.N.T.S. 163. Signed at Seoul July 9, 1966. Entered into force February 9, (continued...)

Philippines

In 1947, the United States and the Republic of the Philippines entered into an agreement on military assistance.[163] The agreement was for a term of five years, starting July 4, 1946, and provided that the United States would furnish military assistance to the Philippines for the training and development of armed forces. The agreement further created an advisory group to provide advice and assistance to the Philippines as had been authorized by the U.S. Congress.[164] The agreement was extended, and amended, for an additional five years in 1953.[165]

A mutual defense treaty was entered into by the United States and the Philippines in 1951.[166] The treaty publicly declares "their sense of unity and their common determination to defend themselves against external armed attack, so that no potential aggressor could be under the illusion that either of them stands alone in the Pacific Area[.]"[167] The Treaty does not address or provide for a SOFA.

The countries entered into a mutual security agreement in 1952,[168] as related to the assurances required by the Mutual Security Act of 1951. The assurances required under the Mutual Security Act of 1951 included a commitment to accounting procedures for monies, equipment, and materials furnished by the United States to the Philippines.[169]

In 1993, the countries entered into a SOFA.[170] The agreement was subsequently extended on September 19, 1994; April 28, 1995; and November 29, December 1, and December 8, 1995. The countries entered into an agreement regarding the treatment of U.S. Armed Forces visiting the Philippines in 1998.[171] The distinction between this agreement and the SOFA originally entered in 1993 is that this agreement applies to U.S. Armed Forces visiting, not stationed in the Philippines. The countries also entered into an agreement regarding the treatment of Republic of Philippines personnel visiting the United States.[172]

(...continued)

1967.

[163] 61 Stat. 3283; T.I.A.S. 1662. Signed at Manila March 21, 1947. Entered into force March 21, 1947.

[164] 61 Stat. 3284.

[165] 4 U.S.T. 1682; T.I.A.S. 2834; 2163 U.N.T.S. 77. Exchange of notes at Manila June 26, 1953. Entered into force July 5, 1953.

[166] 3 U.S.T. 3947; T.I.A.S. 2529; 177 U.N.T.S. 133. Signed at Washington August 30, 1951. Entered into force August 27, 1952.

[167] *Id.*

[168] 3 U.S.T. 4644; T.I.A.S. 2617; 179 U.N.T.S. 193. Exchange of notes at Manila January 4 and 7, 1952. Entered into force January 7, 1952.

[169] *Id.*

[170] Agreement Regarding the Status of U.S. Military and Civilian Personnel, U.S.-Philippines, T.I.A.S. Exchange of notes at Manila April 2, June 11 and 21, 1993. Entered into force June 21, 1993.

[171] Agreement Regarding the Treatment of United States Armed Forces Visiting the Philippines, T.I.A.S. 12931. Signed at Manila February 10, 1998. Entered into force June 1, 1999.

[172] Agreement Regarding the Treatment of Republic of Philippines personnel visiting the United States, T.I.A.S. 12931. Signed at Manila October 9, 1998. Entered into force June 1, 1999.

III. Congressional Oversight

Congress has several tools at its disposal to exercise oversight regarding the negotiation, conclusion, and implementation of international security agreements entered by the United States.

Notification

One manner in which Congress exercises oversight of international agreements is via notification requirements. Obviously, in cases where an agreement requires action from one or both houses of Congress to take effect, notification is a requisite. Before a treaty may become binding U.S. law, the President must submit it to the Senate for its advice and consent. Likewise, the executive must inform Congress when it seeks to conclude an executive agreement that requires congressional authorization and/or implementing legislation to become U.S. law, so that appropriate legislation may be considered.

While constitutional considerations necessitate congressional notification in many circumstances, it has historically been more difficult for Congress to keep informed regarding international agreements or pledges made by the executive that did not require additional legislative action to take effect—that is, sole executive agreements and executive agreements made pursuant to a treaty. Additionally, even in cases where congressional action is necessary for an agreement to take effect, the executive has sometimes opted not to inform Congress about an agreement until it has already been drafted and signed by the parties. In response to these concerns, Congress has enacted legislation and the State Department has implemented regulations to ensure that Congress is informed of the conclusion (and in some cases, the negotiation) of legally binding international agreements.

Notification Pursuant to the Case-Zablocki Act

The Case-Zablocki Act[173] was enacted in 1972 in response to congressional concern that a number of secret agreements had been entered by the executive imposing significant commitments upon the United States.[174] It is the primary statutory mechanism used to ensure that Congress is informed of international agreements entered by the United States. Pursuant to the act, all executive agreements are required to be transmitted to Congress within 60 days of their *entry into force*.[175] If the President deems the immediate public disclosure of an agreement to be prejudicial to national security, the agreement may instead be transmitted to the House Committee on Foreign Affairs and the Senate Committee on Foreign Relations. The President is also required to annually submit a report regarding international agreements that were transmitted after the expiration of the 60-day period, describing the reasons for the delay.[176]

Although the Case-Zablocki Act originally only imposed reporting requirements with respect to executive agreements that had *entered into force*, the act was amended in 2004 to ensure that Congress was regularly notified regarding the status of signed agreements which have yet to enter

---

[173] 1 U.S.C. §112b.

[174] *See* H.Rept. 92-1301, 92nd Cong. (1972).

[175] 1 U.S.C. §112b(a).

[176] *Id.* at §112b(b).

force, as well. The Secretary of State is required to annually report to Congress a list of executive agreements which (1) have not been or are not proposed to be published in the United States Treaties and Other International Agreements compilation and (2) the United States has "signed, proclaimed, or with reference to which any other final formality has been executed, or that has been extended or otherwise modified, during the preceding calendar year."[177]

The Case-Zablocki Act does not define what sort of arrangements constitute "international agreements" falling under its purview, though the legislative history suggests that Congress "did not want to be inundated with trivia ... [but wished] to have transmitted all agreements of any significance."[178] In its implementing regulations, the State Department has established criteria for determining whether an arrangement constitutes a legally binding "international agreement" requiring congressional notification. These include

- the identity of the parties, and whether they intended to create a legally binding agreement;

- the significance of the agreed-upon arrangement, with "[m]inor or trivial undertakings, even if couched in legal language and form," not considered to fall under the purview of the Case-Zablocki Act;

- the specificity of the arrangement;

- the necessity that the arrangement constitute an agreement by two or more parties; and

- the form of the arrangement, to the extent that it helps to determine whether the parties intended to enter a legally binding agreement.[179]

Notification Pursuant to Circular 175 Procedures

The State Department's Circular 175 procedure also contemplates that Congress will be notified of developments in the *negotiation* of "significant" international agreements. Specifically, department regulations provide that

> With the advice and assistance of the Assistant Secretary for Legislative Affairs, the appropriate congressional leaders and committees are advised of the intention to negotiate significant new international agreements, consulted concerning such agreements, and kept informed of developments affecting them, including especially whether any legislation is considered necessary or desirable for the implementation of the new treaty or agreement.[180]

Annual Reporting of Security Arrangements Required by the National Defense Authorization Act of 1991

In addition to the Case-Zablocki Act, Congress has on occasion enacted legislation designed to ensure that it remains informed about existing U.S. security arrangements. Section 1457 of the

---

[177] *Id.* at §112b(d).

[178] H.Rept. 92-1301, 92nd Cong. (1972).

[179] 22 C.F.R. §181.2(a).

[180] 11 F.A.M. §725.1(5).

National Defense Authorization Act for FY1991 (P.L. 101-510) requires the President to submit an annual report to specified congressional committees regarding "United States security arrangements with, and commitments to, other nations."[181] The report, produced in classified and unclassified form, is to be submitted by February 1 each year to the Committee on Armed Services and the Committee on Foreign Relations of the Senate, and the Committee on Armed Services and the Committee on Foreign Affairs of the House of Representatives.[182] In addition to legally binding security arrangements or commitments (e.g., mutual defense treaties and pre-positioning agreements), the report must describe non-binding commitments, such as expressed U.S. policy formulated by the executive branch. It must also include, among other things, "[a]n assessment of the need to continue, modify, or discontinue each of those arrangements and commitments in view of the changing international security situation."[183]

Although reports were submitted to the appropriate committees pursuant to this statutory requirement in 1991 and 1992, it does not appear that any subsequent reports have been issued. The Federal Reports Elimination and Sunset Act of 1995 (Sunset Act, P.L. 104-66) terminated many reporting requirements existing prior to its enactment. The act eliminated or modified several specific reporting requirements, and also generally terminated any reporting requirement that had been listed in House Doc. 103-7, unless such a requirement was specifically exempted. However, the reporting requirement contained in Section 1457 of the FY1991 National Defense Authorization Act was neither specifically terminated by the Sunset Act nor listed in House Doc. 103-7. Moreover, Congress has twice amended Section 1457 after the enactment of the Sunset Act, in 1996 and 1999.[184] Accordingly, it does not appear that this requirement has been terminated.

Consultation

State Department regulations requiring consultation with Congress regarding significant international agreements may provide a means for congressional oversight as to the negotiation of security arrangements. One of the stated objectives of the Circular 175 procedure is to ensure that "timely and appropriate consultation is had with congressional leaders and committees on treaties and other international agreements."[185] To that end, State Department regulations contemplate congressional consultation regarding the conduct of negotiations to secure significant international agreements.[186]

Circular 175 procedures may also provide for congressional consultation concerning the form that a legally binding international agreement should take. When there is question as to whether an international agreement should be entered as a treaty or an executive agreement, the matter is first brought to the attention of the State Department's Legal Adviser for Treaty Affairs. If the Assistant Legal Adviser for Treaty Affairs believes the issue to be "a serious one that may warrant

---

[181] 50 U.S.C. §404c(a).

[182] *Id.* at §404c(c)-(d).

[183] *Id.*

[184] National Defense Authorization Act for Fiscal Year 1996, P.L. 104-106, Div A, §1502(c)(4)(C) (rearranging and revising provisions §1457 of the 1991 National Defense Authorization Act); National Defense Authorization Act for Fiscal Year 2000, P.L. 106-65, Div A, §1067(10) (amending §1457 to reflect name change of House Committee on National Security to House Committee on Armed Services).

[185] 11 F.A.M. §722(4).

[186] *Id.* at §725.1(5).

formal congressional consultation,"[187] consultations are to be held with appropriate congressional leaders and committees. State Department regulations specify that "every practicable effort will be made to identify such questions at the earliest possible date so that consultations may be completed in sufficient time to avoid last minute consideration."[188]

Approval, Rejection, or Conditional Approval of International Agreements

Perhaps the clearest example of congressional oversight in the agreement-making context is through its consideration of treaties and congressional-executive agreements. For a treaty to become binding U.S. law, it must first be approved by a two-thirds majority in the Senate. The Senate may, in considering a treaty, condition its consent on certain reservations, declarations, and understandings concerning treaty application. For example, it may make its acceptance contingent upon the treaty being interpreted as requiring implementing legislation to take effect, or condition approval on an amended version of the treaty being accepted by other treaty parties.[189] If accepted, these reservations, declarations, and understandings may limit and/or define U.S. obligations under the treaty.

As previously discussed, a congressional-executive agreement requires congressional authorization via a statute passed by both houses of Congress. Here, too, approval may be conditional. Congress may opt to authorize only certain types of agreements, or may choose to approve only some provisions of a particular agreement. In authorizing an agreement, Congress may impose additional statutory requirements upon the executive (e.g., reporting requirements). Congress may also include a statutory deadline for its authorization of an agreement to begin or expire.

Because sole executive agreements do not require congressional authorization to take effect, they need not be approved by Congress to become binding, at least as a matter of international law. Nonetheless, as discussed earlier, Congress may limit the effect of a sole executive agreement through a subsequent legislative enactment or through the conditioning of appropriations necessary for the agreement's commitment to be implemented.[190] Similar measures could also be taken to limit or condition U.S. adherence to a non-binding security arrangement.

---

[187] 11 F.A.M. §724.4(b)-(c).

[188] *Id.* at §724.4(b).

[189] In 2007, for instance, the Executive negotiated and signed treaties with the United Kingdom and Australia concerning the export of defense articles, both of which included language in their preambles stating that the treaties were self-executing for the United States. Treaty with the United Kingdom Concerning Defense Trade Cooperation, preamble, SEN. TREATY DOC. 110-7, entered into force April 13, 2012 ("*Understanding* that the provisions of this Treaty are self-executing in the United States ..."); Treaty with Australia Concerning Defense Trade Cooperation, Treaty with the United Kingdom Concerning Defense Trade Cooperation, preamble, SEN. TREATY DOC. 110-10, entered into force April 13, 2012 ("*Understanding* that the provisions of this Treaty are self-executing in the United States ..."). However, the Senate conditioned its approval of both treaties on declarations that they were not self-executing, notwithstanding the language in the agreements' preambles. 156 CONG REC. S7719, 7772, and 7724 (September 29, 2010).

[190] In the 110th Congress, legislation was introduced that would have prohibited appropriations from being used to carry out any U.S.-Iraqi security agreement that was not approved by the Senate as a treaty or authorized by legislation passed by both houses of Congress. *See, e.g.,* S. 2426 (Congressional Oversight of Iraq Agreements Act of 2007); H.R. 4959 (Iraq Strategic Agreement Review Act of 2008); H.R. 5626 (the Protect Our Troops and Our Constitution Act of 2008).

Implementation of an Agreement That Is Not Self-Executing

Congress may exercise oversight regarding international agreements via legislation implementing the agreements' requirements. Certain international treaties or executive agreements are considered "self-executing," meaning that they have the force of law without the need for subsequent congressional action.[191] However, many other treaties and agreements are not considered self-executing, and are understood to require implementing legislation to take effect, as enforcing U.S. agencies otherwise lack authority to conduct the actions required to ensure compliance with the international agreement.[192]

Treaties and executive agreements have, in part or in whole, been found to be non-self-executing for at least three reasons: (1) implementing legislation is constitutionally required; (2) the Senate, in giving consent to a treaty, or Congress, by resolution, requires implementing legislation for the agreement to be given force;[193] or (3) the agreement manifests an intention that it shall not become effective as domestic law without the enactment of implementing legislation.[194]

Until implementing legislation is enacted, existing domestic law concerning a matter covered by an international agreement that is not self-executing remains unchanged and is controlling law in the United States. However, when a treaty is ratified or an executive agreement is entered, the United States acquires obligations under international law and may be in default of those obligations unless implementing legislation is enacted.[195] Perhaps for this reason, Congress typically appropriates funds necessary to carry out U.S. obligations under international agreements.[196]

Continuing Oversight

After an international agreement has taken effect, Congress may still exercise oversight over executive implementation. It may require the executive to submit information to Congress or congressional committees regarding U.S. implementation of its international commitments. It may enact new legislation that modifies or repudiates U.S. adherence or implementation of an international agreement. It may limit or prohibit appropriations necessary for the executive to implement the provisions of the agreement, or condition such appropriations upon the executive implementing the agreement in a particular manner.

---

[191] For purposes of domestic law, a self-executing agreement may be superseded by either a subsequently enacted statute or a new self-executing agreement. *Whitney*, 124 U.S. at 194.

[192] *See generally* RESTATEMENT, *supra* note 13, §111(4)(a) & cmt. h.

[193] For example, in the case of the United Nations Convention Against Torture and Other Cruel, Inhuman or Degrading Treatment or Punishment, G.A. Res. 39/46, Annex, 39 U.N. GAOR Supp. No. 51, U.N. Doc. A/39/51 (1984), the Senate gave advice and consent subject to a declaration that the treaty was not self-executing. U.S. Reservations, Declarations, and Understandings to the Convention Against Torture and Other Cruel, Inhuman or Degrading Treatment or Punishment, 136 CONG. REC. S17486-01 (daily ed., October 27, 1990).

[194] RESTATEMENT, *supra* note 13, §111(4)(a) & n. 5-6.

[195] *See id.*, §111, cmt. h.

[196] *See* TREATIES AND OTHER INTERNATIONAL AGREEMENTS, *supra* note 4, at 166-170 (discussing congressional use of the appropriations power to influence the implementation of international agreements by the United States).

Author Contact Information

Michael John Garcia
Legislative Attorney
mgarcia@crs.loc.gov, 7-3873

R. Chuck Mason
Legislative Attorney
rcmason@crs.loc.gov, 7-9294